The Rooftop

By

Tasha Campbell

ISBN: 1-4107-3836-1 (e-book)
ISBN: 1-4107-3835-3 (Paperback)

This book is printed on acid free paper.

1stBooks - rev. 7/28/03

I dedicate this book to some of the strongest women I have ever known.

My Great-Grandmother- Annie Lee Herbert
My Grandmother- Dorothy Brooks
My Mother- Anita Campbell
My Sister- Aisha Campbell
My best friend- Carolyn Gardner

When I try to define the term Strong Black Women- those names are the only definition I can come up with.

Aisha, not bad for someone who has never been west of 125th Street right?

My grandmother left this earth in July 2001. After attending her funeral in New York City, I came back to the place I now call home, Charlotte, North Carolina. Weeks later, R&B singer/ actress, Aaliyah died in a plane accident. And just a few weeks after that, it was Sept.11. Never had the saying, "you only live once." Meant more to me. My Grandmother's death, Aaliyah's death and Sept.11, had a profound effect on me. My Grandmother's death was somewhat expected, Aaliyah's and everyone who lost their lives on September 11 wasn't. It got me to thinking that indeed no one is promised tomorrow. Your given this gift called life and its up to you to make something of it. Aaliyah was put here to entertain and Dorothy Brooks was destined to save five snot nosed young kids from the system. She adopted all five of us when my mother passed. We ranged in ages from 5 months old to 8 years old. My Grandmother wouldn't let the courts separate us. She gave up her life to save ours. Both women accomplished what they were put on the earth to do. Now I must do what it is I was put here to do and that's write- enjoy!!

My baby girl zhane' I love you from the dirt to the moon baby.

Tariq, Stevie and Abdullah, yall make up what's called family. I love yall all!

ROMELO

"Get in nigga!"

"I'm coming! Shit!"

"Where's Ro?"

"Still inside I guess."

"Fuck!"

Nature got out of the stolen black Impala. He ran back to the lobby of his building and mashed the intercom button to apt.5E.

"Who?" a voice asked.

"It's me grams! Buzz me in!" Nature yelled into the silver box.

Suddenly it occurred to him that the lock on the security door had been broken for weeks. He turned, kicked the door open and ran to the elevator. Before he could press the elevator button, the doors opened up. Romelo Jones stepped out.

"What chu was doin?"Nature asked.

"I had to pee."

"You was probably on the roof writing poetry," Nature said in disgust.

He walked swiftly back to the security door and opened it. He was expecting Ro to be right behind him. He turned and saw Romelo still at the elevator tying his sneaker.

"If I didn't know betta, I'd think you was stalling. I know you ain't scared?"

"Naw," Ro said.

1

"Well come the fuck on then, and I thought I told you to put something black on."

Ro looked down at his red Karl Kani sweatshirt and tugged on it. They both ran to the already packed, stolen car. Nature jumped into the driver's seat.

"Yall make room for him!" he instructed.

Ro climbed into the back of the car. He crawled over Saquan and sat between him and Rugged. Rugged held his fists out and waited for Ro to give him some dap.

"Sup little nigga?"

"Nuthin," Ro replied while slamming his fist down on top of Rugged's.

"Aiiight chall let's do this," Nature said as he pulled the car out of its parking space.

The streets were pretty empty for a Sunday night in the Bronx. They rode in silence, eyes peeled to the streets, except Ro. He fidgeted, kept tapping his right hand on his right knee, and kept kicking the seat in front of him.

"Nigga if you kick this seat one more time…" Lee said from the front seat.

Nature peered at Ro through the rear view mirror.

"He scared," Lee said.

"No he ain't, that's a tough little ma fucka right there," Rugged said.

Nature looked at Romelo though the rear view again.

"Memba when he pushed that fat kid off his bike?"

Laughter erupted.

"Hell yea!" Saquan said. "He told dat kid, now you lay right there. I'm gon ride your bike and when I get

2

tired you can have it back. But don't you get your fat ass up until I do."

The whole car roared with laughter again.

"But this is different," Lee said.

Silence took over.

Nature drove another few blocks and then stopped at the corner of Thornwood Avenue. Lee sat up and pulled a blunt from out of his sock. He lit it and took a long pull. Ro looked out the window, he squinted his eyes trying to read the number to the house they were parked in front of. When he gave up trying, he kicked the seat in front of him. Nature turned around quickly.

"Would you chill wit dat!" he yelled at Ro.

"He scared." Lee said while passing the blunt to Nature.

Nature took two quick pulls and let the smoke work its way into his system; he then slowly let the smoke out. Ro watched the smoke hit the roof of the car then spread out. Nature looked out the car window, up the block, and then he looked out at the rear view mirror, down the block. Nothing, no one, not a soul in sight. "Perfect," he thought.

"You should be the last one calling someone scared," he said while looking at Lee.

"When dem niggas caught yo ass at the video store wit yo moms, your bitch ass ran."

Saquan and Rugged broke out in laughter.

"Wouldn't you? Shit!" Lee said.

Nature reached over the front seat and passed the blunt to Rugged.

"I'm sayin, you got seven niggas standing in front of you and they flashing straight razors and box

3

cutters. You gon stand there?" Lee asked sounding frustrated.

"I'm gon protect my moms," Rugged said while holding in the smoke until he couldn't hold it any longer. He blew it towards the small crack in the window. Romelo saw the cloud approaching him; he tried to hold his breath so as not to take any of it in. But it was no use; every time he took a small breath, weed smoke was ingested.

"Man…Fuck yall! My moms was on the other side of the store. She didn't even know what was goin down. Far as she knew I just bounced on her."
Rugged brushed the ashes he dropped on his legs off. He looked at Ro and asked," You want?" He held the half smoked blunt in his face.

"Don't give him none. He only 8," Lee said.

"So?" Nature said. "That's how old I was when I started."

"True…me too," Rugged chimed in.

"His ass shouldn't even be here," Lee said while scowling at Ro.

Romelo took the blunt from Rugged, held it for a second, and then passed it over to Saquan.

"Man, you getting on my nerves. Why? Why shouldn't he be here? This a part of us. This our history, this our life!" Nature yelled. "This shits been going on since I was his age and before that"

"Hell yea," added Saquan.

"Dem niggas been fuckin wit us for years!" Nature yelled.

"Word!" Rugged said. "My older brother can tell you. Shit he can show you. He got the battle scars. It's just been passed down from them to us."

4

"I know…I"m just sayin…" Lee said.

"What chu sayin? Huh?!! Nothing! You ain't sayin shit!" said Nature.

"Everybody knows, niggas who live in Foster Houses don't fuck with niggas who live in Vector houses. It's as simple as that."

"Ro might as well get used to it cause the younger generation gonna come up with da same shit," Saquan said.

"Fucking dumb ass done blew my high. Pass dat blunt man," Nature said while he turned on the car stereo. Ro just sat back, looked and listened. He knew about the Vector and Foster war but only what he heard Nature and his friends discuss. He really didn't care about who went to what school or who was seen on what playground. He did know that he wasn't allowed to go no where near Vector and that his friend Trevor was jumped by a bunch of 10 year olds after school last week just because he lived in Foster. Nature picked the tape he had sitting on the dashboard up and put it in.

"Yall niggas be quiet," he said.

He pressed play and they all sat in silence while the words of KRS ONE, and smoke from the blunt filled the air. Romelo bobbed his head back and forth while he mouthed the words to Criminal Minded. He didn't need to put the blunt to his lips and pull. The smoke in the car was giving him a contact. He started feeling a little less nervous. He looked at Nature, who was sitting with his eyes closed, moving his head back and forth. He wondered what Nature was thinking at this very moment. He then glanced at Lee and as if Lee was reading his mind, he turned and looked at Ro. Ro caught Lee's glare and quickly turned away. He turned to his right and looked at Saquan. Sa was holding his pager up close to his eyes, scanning through the numbers he had stored. Finally he turned to Rugged; he was finishing off what was left of the blunt. They sat there like that forever or so it seemed to Romelo, but that was cool he thought. Because he really didn't want to do anything else except maybe go home and play basketball with his friends or play Nintendo.

Nature opened his eyes and asked what time it was.

"11:58," Lee answered.

"K...'nuff bullshitin, lets go."

He turned off the tape player, reached under his seat and pulled out a large object wrapped in a white towel. Romelo stretched his neck trying to get a better view. Then Rugged reached under the seat in front of him and pulled out what looked like a rifle. Saquan leaned over and passed Rugged a small box.

"What's that? Ro asked.

"Family enders," Rugged replied.

"Word," said Saquan with a chuckle. "Put an end to your whole family."

Ro watched as Rugged pulled two red and white objects from out of the box Saquan had just given him.

"Is that a rifle?" he asked in a hushed voice.

"A sawed off kid."

Ro looked at the objects Rugged had placed on his lap. He then heard a snap, he thought Rugged had broken the sawed off because it appeared to be in two pieces.

"Hand me the bullets."

Ro picked up the bullets, gave them to Rugged and watched as he loaded them down the barrel of the sawed off rifle. The start of the car engine made Ro jump and automatically he felt nervous again. Rugged snapped the sawed off back into one piece and laid it on his lap. Nature put the car in drive and slowly inched along. The streets in Vector remained quiet with the exception of a few dog barks here and there. Nature didn't bother to turn on the headlights to the car as they crept slowly along.

"Is that it?"Saquan asked.

"Does it say 3210?" Nature asked while peering out the window.

"Yea…dats it."

Nature stopped the car a couple of houses up from 3210. He pulled his black champion sweat hood off and threw it to Ro in the back seat.

"Put that on."

"It's too big."

"I said put it on. I told you to wear something black."

Romelo sucked his teeth, and then pulled the sweat hood over his head.

"And keep the hood on," Nature told him. He got out of the car but left the engine running and the door open. Lee got out on his side and put the hood to his sweatshirt on his head. Saquan and Rugged got out and did the same.

"Come on Sa." Nature beckoned to Saquan to get into the drivers seat. Once Saquan was seated behind the wheel, he closed the door quietly. Rugged passed the sawed off to Nature. He walked to the passenger side of the car and reached inside to unlock the glove department. Romelo remained glued to his seat. Nature pulled out a small object and got back out of the car. He then walked to the back door and leaned in.

"Let's go Ro."

Romelo slid across the seat and stepped out of the car. As he stood up, the sweat hood Nature had given him to wear fell into place on him. It hung low, past his knees and the hood hung down to his eyebrows. Nature walked over to him and fixed the sleeves by pulling them up. He then pulled the drawstrings attached to the hood hard enough to make the hood close around Romelos face.

"You aight?" Nature asked him.

"Yea...I guess."

"Don't sweat it lil man, we ain't killin no one. This just revenge for them jumping Mark two weeks ago. You remember I told you bout that right?"

"Yea...Is he still in the hospital?"

"Yea, here this is for you," Nature said as he handed Ro a small black object.

"A gun?" Romelo asked, sounding surprised.

"Um hmm, it's a deuce deuce. Clean, no bodies. It's yours."

Romelo took the gun out of Natures palm and eyed it closely.

"Come on yall," Lee said.

JADA

"Jada Romain, are you still up?"

Jada quietly ran across her bedroom and jumped in her bed. She pulled the sheets up to her neck and squeezed her eyes shut. Her mother opened the bedroom door and stuck her head in. The hallway light shined directly on Jada's face.

"Now that is strange," her mother said while stepping into the room.

"I could have sworn I heard singing coming from in here. Sounded just like Whitney Houston."

"For real?" Jada said as she sat straight up.

"Ah-ha! Knew you weren't asleep."

Jada giggled while her mom sat down on the bed next to her.

"I don't know of any seven year old who would still be up at this time of night. Can't sleep?"

"Not really."

"Nervous about the first day of school tomorrow?"

"I'm just wondering who will be in my class. And I'm also thinking about what I want for my birthday in a couple of days."

"I'm sure you will see some of your friends from your second grade class tomorrow in your third grade class. And we will talk about your birthday later, ok?"

Just then the walls to Jada's bedroom began to rumble.

"That's why I can't sleep, Terry and his stupid friends makin so much noise."

"I've talked to that boy time and time again about blasting that music at this hour. Terrance is about to go walk shep so his company will be leaving out with him."

"Terrance, turn down that music!" Jada heard her father yell from the bedroom across the hall.

"And go walk that dog!"

Jada and her mother listened as Terrance and his friends left his bedroom and headed downstairs.

"Good night Mr. And Mrs. Romain," Terrance best friend, Cancer yelled out.

"Is that better?"

"Yea," Jada answered.

"Good. It's chilly in here honey."

Mrs. Romain walked to the window and closed it. She then walked back to the bed and pulled the covers up to Jada's shoulders.

"Mary! Come here for a sec. you've got to see this replay."

"Alright Reggie."

"He taped the football game?" She asked her mother.

"Umm hmm, and I have to go and act like I care."

They both laughed as Mary bent to kiss her daughter on the cheek.

"Love you."

"I love you too mommy."

The minute her mother closed the bedroom door, Jada kicked the covers off her. She closed her eyes and turned on her side. She tried to fall asleep but it was no good, she couldn't. She jumped out the bed and walked towards the window. Jada picked the Winnie the Pooh stuffed doll that was sitting on the windowsill up and held it in one hand while she opened the window with the other. Jada looked out the window and saw four people stop in front of her house. At first she thought it was her brother and his friends but when she didn't recognize any of the faces, she knew it couldn't have been them. One of them looked like a little boy, she thought. She sunk to her knees and watched the only person in the group who wasn't wearing a hood on his head; lift the latch on the gate in front of the house. He pulled his baseball cap down further on his head and then pulled his right arm out from behind his back. At this time the others pulled their hands either from out of their pockets or from their sides. Jada watched the youngest one as he held a small black object with both his hands. She moved closer to the window, almost sticking her head out. It was then that she realized what the youngest one was holding.

"A gun?" she whispered.

They walked right up to the front door. Then Jada heard her mom yell.

"I'll get it Reggie, it's probably Terrance. He can never remember to take his house keys with him."

Jada looked at her closed bedroom door; she then looked back out the window. From her view she could now only see two of the guys, both of them had guns in their hands. One guy was shifting his weight from one foot to the other and kept looking up and down the block. Jada got up quickly and ran to her bedroom door. She pulled it open and called for her mother. She looked down the hallway and saw the top of her mother's head as she was descending the steps.

"MOM!" Jada yelled.

"Why aren't you asleep Jay?" her father asked while sticking his head out the bathroom doorway.

"Mom," Jada said as she ran past him still clutching Winnie.

"Mom what? What's wrong?" he asked.

"Mommy don't!" Jada yelled. She ran down the steps as fast as her little seven year old legs would take her.

"Jay, what?!!" Mary asked while placing her hand on the front door knob.

"Ding…Dong"

"Terrance pleaseeee, I'm here…I'm here."

Jada caught up to her mother while she was just about to open the front door. Before she could warn her about anything, shots rang out. Mary Romain screamed. Wood chips from the front door whizzed past her, one grazed her left cheek. Jada screamed and covered her ears, and then suddenly she dropped both arms and fell to the floor. Mary dove at Jada and landed on top of her, she lay there while the noise continued.

"What the hell is going on?" Reggie yelled.

He saw his wife lying on top of his daughter near their front door. The lamp on the front table shattered and Reggie fell to his knees. When the noise came to a halt, he ran down the steps.

"Oh my God, Mary?" he knelt down beside her.

"Mary?" he whispered.

"I'm okay Reggie." Suddenly she realized she was on top of Jada and she jumped up.

"Jada?"

Mary saw blood on the front of Jada's nightgown and screamed.

"Oh lord...Jada, honey?" Reggie noticed Jada's Winnie the Pooh lying on top of her covered in blood. He removed it and noticed a hole in her right shoulder.

"Ahhhhhhh..." Mary screamed.

Reggie placed his arm under Jada's back, the other arm under her legs and scooped her up.

"Mary get the car," he said sounding defeated.

Mary was frantic. She looked at the blood on the floor and screamed again.

"Mary! Get the car, now!" Reggie yelled.

ROMELO

Romelo walked alongside Nature in silence. Nature held the sawed off shotgun behind his back. Ro did the same with the twenty-two. Once they got in front of 3210, Saquan backed the car up slowly and sat waiting.

"Here it is," Nature said.

Nature pulled his baseball cap down further on his head. He stepped up to the fence and lifted the hatch. He walked towards the front door, Lee, Ro and Rugged followed. Ro cupped the gun in both his hands. Nature stopped in front of the door.

"I'm gonna ring da doorbell, then we shoot. Just bring the door down."

"What if someone comes to answer it?"Ro asked.

"We shoot before they do," Nature answered.

"And if they do? Oh fuckin well," said Lee.

"Ring da bell Ro," Nature instructed.

Ro walked up to the lit button on the doorframe and pressed his thumb down on it. A car came down the street at the same exact time.

"Wait...wait till it passes," said Nature.

The car passed Saquan slowly then sped up to the corner and made a left.

"Ok press it again," Said Lee.

Ro pressed it for the second time. Voices from inside the house were heard. What sounded like a little girl, yelled out for her mother. And then a woman's voice was overheard saying;'I'm here...I'm here."

"Now!" yelled Lee.

All four boys raised their guns and shot at the door. Romelo squeezed his right pointer finger on the trigger and closed his eyes tight. He heard Lee yelling, "Yea mutha fuckas!" Ro just kept his eyes shut. The noise was deafening to him. He stopped shooting only because he felt Natures arm come down on his.

"Let's go!" Rugged yelled.

Ro opened his eyes and looked at the front door to house 3210. There were small holes and there were large holes. It looks like Swiss cheese Ro thought. There was smoke in the air and lights from other houses were being switched on. Nature grabbed Ro by the arm and they ran to the waiting Impala. Lee jumped in the front and slammed the door. Nature, Ro and Rugged jumped in the back. Rugged slammed the door and Saquan pulled off. At first no one said anything, they sat in silence. Saquan entered onto the Cross Bronx Expressway, heading towards Manhattan. Once on the expressway Saquan let out a loud laugh.

"Oh shit!" he said while holding his left fist up to his mouth.

Nature and Rugged began to laugh also. Lee just looked out the window and kept repeating the word "yea" over and over again. Romelo looked at the gun he still held in his hand. He wanted to drop it, better yet throw it in the river. He never wanted to see it again. But of course he dare not tell Nature or any of the rest of them this.

"Let's dump this somewhere in Manhattan, and catch the train back," said Nature.

"Fuck Vector," Lee said.

"Yea...fuck dem niggas," Saquan added.

"Yo say pump dat tape."

Saquan pressed play; automatically they all started bobbing their heads back and forth.

"Criminal minded you've been blinded…" Nature sang out.

"Shit! What time is it?" he asked.

Saquan looked at his beeper then replied;' almost one."

"Damn. First day of school."

They dumped the stolen car in Harlem. All four of them walked to the train station, hoped the 6 train and rode it to the Bronx.

Romelo missed his first day of 3rd grade because he and Nature simply overslept.

Jada missed her first three weeks of 3rd grade and celebrated her 8th birthday recovering from a bullet wound that came from a .22 caliber weapon, which entered and exited her right shoulder.

8 years later

"Past me the rock baby!"Romelo yelled.

His homeboy Trevor dribbled the ball and shot Ro a quick look. He immediately faked his defender out by looking to his left but passing the ball to Ro on his right. Ro caught the ball, looked down to the ground to make sure he was at the 3pt. Line. He squared up, raised his arms and let the ball go. Swish…all net.

"Yea baby!" he yelled, arms still raised.

Trevor walked over to him and gave him a pound.

"Dat's what I'm talking bout!"

They exchanged handshakes and elbow taps with their opponents. Tre and Ro picked up their tee shirts and crawled thru the hole in the wire link fence that separated the schoolyard from the street. They stopped and exchanged a few more brotherly shows of affection with some people who were sitting on top of a parked car.

"I saw that kid!!"Said one.

"You headed to the NBA," said another.

The streetlights came on, which in Foster houses meant that in another ten to fifteen minutes almost all of the stores would be closed, with the exception of Bobby's Deli. Bobby's door would be locked but one could still do business by talking thru a few holes fixed in three inch Plexiglas, and by placing money on a circular table that can be turned around to face the night manager. He would then take your money and place what you wanted along with your change back on the round table and spin. Thus creating an opening for you to retrieve your items.

Trevor said," You want something from Bobby's before he lock the doors?"

"Naw I'm cool. I've been pigging out all summer. Got to go on a strict diet. First day of school tomorrow and coach already got us on two hour practices after school."

"Word?"Tre asked.

"Yea man."

Romelo looked up the street as they started to head for their building, and spotted Calvin sitting on the wall, along with some of his other cronies.

"Fuck they doin ova here?"Tre asked.

"I don't know. I heard Keisha who live in C building is messing with Cancer."

"For real?"

"S'what I heard."

"That's some shit," Tre said while eyeing Calvin.

"Yo, let's cut thru the alley," said Ro while he and Tre dashed across the street. Soon as Tre stepped up onto the sidewalk a burgundy Nissan screeched up beside him. Ro and Tre turned around quickly. Butta stepped out and started laughing.

"Dang!! Yall should have seen yall faces."

"Yall looked all shook and shit," Lil Mickey said while slamming the back passenger door.

They all exchanged daps and hugs. Ro peeked in the car and waved to Aisha, butta's girl.

"Hey Trevor, sup Romeo?"

Tre, Lil Mickey and Butta laughed.

"He ain't no Romeo," exclaimed Butta. "Shit...my sista get more of the nappy snappy then he do."

"That's cause your sister is gay nigga. And she fine as hell too," said Tre.

Butta walked over to the driver's side and leaned in and gave Aisha a kiss.

"Yall headed home?" he asked afterwards.

"Yea," they said in unison.

"Aight. Yo boo I'm a walk with them. Page me lata."

"Kool."

Aisha rolled up her window and sped off down the street blasting Mary J. Blige.

"Who car she driving?"Tre asked.

"Her moms, she be stealing the car keys."

"You should call her ass speed racer," Romelo said.

"Tell me that's not Calvin and them sitting ova there on the wall?"Lil Mickey asked in disbelievement.

"Yea, that's him."

Butta turned to face Calvin and his crew of two. Calvin noticed, stood up and locked looks with Butta.

"Come on man," Ro said.

Butta backed up slowly and finally turned around and caught up with them.

"Calvin ain't the reason why yall cutting thru the alley is it?"Butta asked.

There was a short period of silence, and then finally from Ro, "I'm just tired of it. That's all. I got other shit on my mind. This my junior year, I got one more year of high school after that I'm going to college…"

"If the NBA doesn't snatch your ass up first," Tre interrupted.

"Them fools ain't on my mind," Ro said.

"I hear you…but I'm sayin tho how come it is they can bring they broke asses round our way, chill and talk to these girls over here and then the next night come back shooting up the mutha fucka? Yet we can't even step foot in Vector?"

"Well, I don't wanna chill ova there anyway," Lil Mickey, said.

"Me either but I bet if we did, all hell would break loose."

"Tings been eesee for a minute now star," Ro said in a fake Jamaican accent.

They all broke out in laughter.

"Yea it's been quiet but still…you know dem niggas."

Ro, Butta, Tre and Lil Mickey walked the rest of the way home in silence. They approached the building in which they lived from behind. Foster Houses was made up of three different kinds of buildings. Single core, double core and tri-core. It was one of the huge tri-core buildings in Foster in which Romelo and his friends lived. It was separated by three sections, the A building is where Ro and Butta lived. B building was in the middle and that's where Lil Mickey lived. C building was on the end, that's the building Tre lived in. Each building had twenty-six floors and was attached by taking the elevator down to the basement and walking through to another building. When Romelo and Nature were younger, they used to go to the basement all the time and "explore". It was creepy to Ro; he imagined all sorts of monsters lived down there. They would play hide and seek or write graffiti on the walls. When Nature got older he would take girls down to the basement and smoke weed with them and feel up on them or if they was willing and high enough, have sex. Nature said it was cheaper then a hotel room. 'A forty and a blunt, is all they really want," he would say. "Once you give em that, they yours for at least the next 10-15 mins."

All of them walked to the front of C building. Butta and Ro gave Lil Mickey and Tre dap.

"See you lata dog," Ro said while standing in front of Trevor.

"Say word," Tre said as his eyes widened.

"What?" asked Ro.

"Here come dat nigga Cancer."

"Word?"Ro asked still looking Tre in the eyes.

"Yea, he just came out of your building wit Keisha."

"Told you he mess with her."

"That's why Calvin and them was ova here, he never ride alone," Butta said.

Cancer, walking a few steps in front of Keisha, approached them. When he spotted Ro he slowed down a bit.

"Why you walking so damn fast?"Keisha yelled to him.

As Cancer passed Ro and the rest he asked; "where's your punk ass brother Nature?"

Ro didn't answer he just met Cancers glare with his own.

"Wait up!"Keisha yelled.

He turned to look at her.

"Come da fuck on."

He then looked back at the 4 of them and smiled.

"See yall lata…trust."

And with that his smile faded. He headed towards his cream colored Acura that was parked in front of C building. Keisha began to run in order to keep up with him. As she passed Ro, she screwed up her lips and rolled her eyes at the four.

"Did she just roll her eyes at us?"Butta asked.

"Fuck she see in him?"Ro wondered out loud.

"Hell, what da fuck he see in her?"Lil Mickey asked.

"That's messed up. She gon git hers tho. Stank hoe. She be the one calling them niggas, telling em when we outside playin ball or chillin on da wall," Tre said.

"See that's the shit I'm talking about," Butta said sounding frustrated.

"How she gonna play all us like that. But let us go ova to Vector and mack one of dem gurls ova there.

They know we from Foster, they won't give us the time of day."

Butter kicked a rock that was lying in front of him so hard that it skidded down the sidewalk and hit a garbage can.

"Yo yall, forget Keisha and forget Vector. I'm out."

And with that, Ro gave Tre, Butta and Lil Mickey some dap and walked to A building. Romelo entered apartment 5e and headed straight to the kitchen. He pulled open the stove door and looked in, a baked ham looked back at him. He closed the stove and decided to pour himself a bowl of applejacks. Ro's sister entered the kitchen.

"Sup Ro?"

"What's up?"

"Grama cooked you know," Tanaesha said.

"I know, don't feel like eating dinner right now tho."

"Well shit I'm gonna eat," she said while dishing out some macaroni and cheese.

"You always eating."

"It's not me who's hungry, it's the baby."

"Yea okay."

Romelo got up and put his bowl in the kitchen sink. He then reached over and rubbed Tanesha's stomach.

"Stop...I hate that," she said.

"You decide what college you going to after you graduate this year?" he asked her.

"Dang Ro, school ain't even start yet."

"I know but still...I know where I wanna go. I wanna play for the Tar heels so I'm going to North Carolina."

"Well first make it thru highschool," she said while chewing on some ham. Just then Nature walked into the kitchen.

"Who's going to North Cakalac?"He asked.

"When I graduate, I am." Ro started bouncing the basketball on the kitchen floor. He then balanced it on his pointer finger and gave it a spin.

"Nigga you ain't goin no where."

Nature grabbed the ball and began dribbling it himself.

"If he says he going to NC, then he is going. Just because you didn't finish high school…"

"Shut up, ain't nobody talking to you. And stop feeding that baby swine," Nature said to Tanaesha.

"Yea…ummmm Ro was talking to me so you shut up," she said as she rolled her eyes at him.

"Anyway…Ro, Ebony called, said she will call you back and some other chick called," Nature said.

Tanaesha let out a loud belch.

"Pig!" Nature shot at her.

"Punk!" she shot back. Ro just laughed and grabbed the ball from Nature. Suddenly he stopped dribbling and looked at him.

"Cancer just asked me bout you."

"When? Where you see him at?"

"Right outside C building."

"Are you serious?"

"He goes wit Kiesha," Tanaeasha said.

"Yea…Calvin and them was chillin on the wall earlier to," Ro said.

"Fuck! I hope they not tryin to start shit up again. I just finished doing 9 months for some petty bullshit."

"I don't even know why Cancer hang with Calvin and Rayson. Calvin is Ro's age and Cancer what? 24? 25?" Tanaesha asked.

"Cancer 23, a year older than me," said Nature.

"He punk."

The doorbell rang. Ro walked over to it and peered thru the peephole.

"Who is it?"

"Rugged," the voice outside answered.

Ro opened up and let Rugged in.

"Sup nigga."

"Ain't nuthin," Rugged replied. He gave Ro a hug and some dap. Nature stepped out of the kitchen and received a pound from Rugged too.

"What's in the bag yo?"

"Some baby stuff. Here Nae Nae. And Ro I got you some new kicks for the first day of school tomorrow. Them new black and white Jordan's you wanted."

"Awww shit, lemme see."

"What you get me daddy?" Nature joked.

"Nuthin, your ass grown, buy your own shit." Ro tried on his new sneakers and grinned hard.

"Good looking Rugged," he said.

"No doubt, yall fam. Where's grams?"

"In the back, sleeping," Nae Nae said while holding up a white and yellow terry cloth bib that read, 'SPIT HAPPENS.' She walked over to Rugged and gave him a kiss on his lips.

"That's how yall got in this mess now," Ro joked.

Rugged had become the neighbor hood drug dealer. After shooting up the door to house 3210 eight years ago, a full-scale war between Vector and Foster houses jumped off. Terrance and his homeboys got home from walking shep to find neighbors and police standing on the front lawn and going in and out of the house. When a neighbor informed him that his little sister had gotten shot, he jetted to Our Lady of Mercy hospital to check on her. Once he found out that she was indeed still alive, his fear turned to outrage. He rounded up 4 of his homies from Vector and three months after they shot his door down, Foster complex was hit. On a 50-degree winter afternoon, shortly after school had let out, 4 guys opened fire on a crowd of highschoolers as they stood around. Most of the crowd was from Foster. Kelly Hale, whose family had moved from Foster the previous year, had rolled thru that day just to check out his home boys. He was hit twice in the back. Kelly was pronounced dead at the scene. Omar Taylor, who had come to Foster to visit his girlfriend Priscilla, was shot in his left ankle and calf. He ran all the way to Priscilla's crib and didn't realize he was hit until he sat down to tell her what had happened and noticed blood on his sneaker. He was taken to the hospital and had one of the two bullets removed. Omar continues to this day to walk with a limp. Saquan Goodmoore had just finished talking to Omar and was headed to Nature's crib. As he was about to cross the street, he thought he heard someone call his name. He turned and looked but didn't see anyone calling him. He continued to walk on but was stopped by Mrs. Robinson. He asked her about her son, and when was he getting out. Then he heard it again, someone was calling his name. He looked towards the wall and then the basketball courts. Just past the courts, way in the back, standing in front of G building, stood Terence. Mrs. Robinson was going on and on, telling him about her son and how he was going to become a new father soon but Saquan tuned her out. Terrance began walking in their direction. He opened the black leather trench coat he was wearing revealing a shiny silver gun that was protruding from the waist of his black jeans. Terrance made no attempt to conceal his weapon or his face as he walked faster towards the heavy populated Foster shopping area. Saquan turned and looked Mrs. Robinson in the eyes.

"Run," he said simply. But before she could understand or even ask what he meant by that, shots rang out. The crowd scattered like roaches when a kitchen light is turned on. Saquan began to run towards A building, when he turned to get a visual on Terrance he saw Mrs. Robinson on the ground. She was the third casualty that day. She died of a single gunshot wound to the neck. When Saquan turned back around he saw a dark-skinned kid standing a few paces in front of him. He couldn't remember his name but he knew this kid hung with Terrance. Saquan stopped in his tracks and just stared. Cancer stood there with the same long black leather trench on; a pair of black shades covered his eyes. He knew Terrance had said he wanted to be the one to off Saquan because he was certain he was the one parked outside his home the night his baby sister was shot. A homeboy of his named Greg had passed Saquan in his car while Saquan sat and waited for Nature and the rest. But Cancer had an itchy trigger finger and couldn't wait on Terrance. He untied the belt on his coat and pulled out a glock. He held the glock up and pointed it towards Saquan.

The morning newspaper read, 'THREE DEAD, FIVE INJURED IN GANG SHOOTING.' Saquan's mother was furious and called the media. She insisted that her son was not a member of any gang; he was just a victim of his environment.

"These little black boys have been killing each other over here for years, yall just don't care. We have begged for more protection and police presence in our community."

Because of the media attention after the deaths, police presence in Foster was stepped up. On the day of Saquan's funeral a police sub station was erected right smack in the middle of Foster. Not just the young kids of Foster but everyone was banned from hanging out after dark at the shopping area or the wall. Rugged and Nature dropped out of Truman high school after Saquan's death. Rugged's father in turn, kicked his only son out of the house.

"No worthless no good nigger is gonna live under my roof and mooch off of me," is what he told him. Rugged moved in with his bestfriend Nature and began to sell drugs in Foster. No arrests were made in the killings of Saquan, Mrs. Robinson and Kelly Hale. Nature, Rugged, Lee and some others who lived there talked about revenge, but eventually things quieted down.

JADA

Jada lay on her bed, feet propped up on the wall. She looked at her poster of L L Cool J and smiled.

"I'm going to become a famous photographer and take pictures of you one day," she said to a smiling L L.

"When you do, can I be there?" her best friend Monica asked while sitting at the foot of Jay's bed, thumbing through Vibe magazine.

"So you're decided on what you wearing tomorrow for the first day of school?" Monica asked her.

"Not yet…probably some jeans I got with the holes in the knees and my black turtleneck and black boots. It's supposed to be a little chilly tomorrow."

"Aight bet," Monica said as she got up off the bed.

"I'm gonna wear my holy jeans too."

Jada swung her legs around and sat up.

"You gonna try out for cheerleader this year Monie"

"No girl, that's you. I'll just be their watching the cuties play and practice, oh and of course to support you."

"Oh of course. I can't believe the first day of school is tomorrow. This summer went too fast," Jada said, then sucked her teeth.

"I can't believe your going to be 16 in a few more days," Monica said excitedly.

"I know, my party is gonna be bomb. I have been planning this for a long time."

"Where's it gonna be at again?"

"We gonna rent out the big room in the community center. I wanted to have it here but my moms said no."

"You should have known that," Monica said. "She barely let your have any company."

"I know," Jada said with a frown. "She's so overprotective."

"Overprotective isn't the word," Monica said.

Jada's mother knocked on her bedroom door then opened it. She walked in and glanced at the Looney tunes clock hanging on the wall.

"Monica it's getting late."

"Ok Mrs. Romain."

"Do you need for me and Jay to walk you home?" she asked.

"No ma'am, I'm straight."

"Ok honey. Jay don't stay up too late."

"I'm not mommy, I'm just gonna walk Monie down stairs."

Mary walked over to Jada's bedroom window and peeped out. After taking in a deep breath she turned around to face the girls.

"Ok...see you in the morning then. You're wearing your new outfit tomorrow right?"

"Ewwww," both girls said.

"Mommy, no one wears their new clothes on the first day of school."

Jada's mother laughed. "What? The second day?"

"Try the second week maybe," Monica said.

"Monica you be careful walking home...and you call Jay soon as you get there."

"Ok Mrs. Romain."

Jada's mother left the room. The girls looked at each other.

"She still trip out round this time of year?" Monica asked.

"She's not as bad as she used to be but...yea. She still checks the window every night."

"My moms would probably act the same way."

"Your moms would be worst," Jada said. They both laughed and agreed to that. Monica put her arm around Jada and Jay did the same to her best friend. They walked down the steps like that and headed to the front door.

"Oh Jay!! You got to add Derek to the invite list."

"Derek? Why Derek?"

"Causeeeeeee!! He is sooo cute! Oh and invite ummm..."

"We can go over the guest list again together Monie," Jay said while opening the front door.

"Cool." Monica stepped outside, while Jada leaned against the door's frame.

"Jay?"

"Huh?"

"You think your pops is gonna come to your party?"

"I don't know Monie. I hope so..."

After Jada had gotten shot her mother blamed Terrance for their "near death" experience. She became very protective of Jada, even quitting her job as a home attendant so she could stay home. "Be there all the time to protect my only baby girl," is what she told people. This caused her and Reggie to argue about finances. She accused him of "caring about a paycheck more then their daughter." After the deaths in Foster, Reggie sent Terrance to go live with family in Brooklyn because he didn't want any more trouble coming to his door. Terrance stayed in Brownsville all of six months before he was sent back to his parents in the Bronx. Two days after Saquan's funeral, Mark Anderson got out of the hospital. He was happy to be home, back in Foster. He automatically began talk of revenge. Saquan, Mrs. Robinson and Kelly Hale's deaths were still fresh, so no one was ready to hear about more killings. He accused Foster of going soft while he was in the hospital, but what he really was mad at was Vector niggas had put him in there in the first place. And he figured if no one was going to get revenge for it all, he would do it himself. He walked around all the time talking about killing whole families in Vector houses. After awhile people began to say he had lost his mind over Saquan's death. He talked non-stop of revenge. A year had passed since the funerals and Mark was still kicking the revenge rhetoric. One day he caught up with Nature and Romelo as they were headed to A building.

"What up Nature? What up Ro?"

"What up Mark?" Nature said while giving him some dap.

"Man listen, I'm ready to head to Vector tonight, you down Nature? I know yall niggas had my back last time..."

"Mannnn Mark you ain't going to Vector tonight," Nature said.

Just then Rugged and two other cats rolled up.

"That nigga still talking that shit?" Rugged asked.

"When they broke your jaw, you must have hit your head on da concrete," another one interjected.

Laughter rang out.

"Clown me if yall want to…but I'm a carve my fuckin name in Terrance chest." Everyone roared with laughter, this infuriated Mark.

"Come on Ro!" Mark said while grabbing Ro by the collar of his coat.

"I know you down. I heard how your little ass got down last time."

Nature grabbed Mark with both hands and threw him. He stumbled on some snow that lie on the sidewalk and fell.

"Son? Don't ever put your hands on my brother again!" Nature yelled. "I don't know what's wrong with you dog. All you talk bout is killing. You running your mouth too much and mad ears is listening. That's not the way you do things, just shut da fuck up cause you ain't doing shit!"

Nature and Ro walked away from the crowd. The others helped Mark up, he brushed off the snow that stuck to his jacket and walked off yelling how he was going to revenge Saquan. But as much junk as Mark popped, all of a sudden one day he just stopped. He went on and on about the whole thing for a year then suddenly clammed up. People around Foster figured he must have realized he looked and sounded like a nut. The beef with Foster and Vector houses just seemed to end altogether. But for Mark it was far from over, yea he shut up about the whole thing, he just became tired of everyone thinking he had lost his mind. As he sat on a wooden bench at 1 in the morning, in Vector Park, he thought maybe he was losing his mind. He zipped up his Reebok jacket and lit a cigarette.

"No one treats me like that tho, no one," He said out loud. He grabbed his beer and took another swig. "Right Saquan? Yall niggas wanna break my jaw, my nose and think I won't do shit?"He yelled. Mark had already finished one 40oz. Of beer and was working on another. He had two more unopened bottles lined up on the bench next to him along with a pack of Newport's. He knew Terrance like a book by now; after all he had been following him around for weeks. He glanced at his watch, it was close to 2:00 a.m. and he knew Terrance would be walking through Vector Park any minute now. This time Mark wouldn't hide; he sat there many a nights and usually hid in some low brush when Terrance came by.

"Not tonight," he said.

Terrance and Will walked thru the park talking loudly. Each bragged on how much money was in their pockets, how many girls were on their shit and how soon it would be time to re-up. As they approached Mark, he put the beer bottle down and stood up.

"What up Tee? What up Will?"

Terrance and Will stopped and looked Mark in the eyes.

"I know you patna?"Will asked.

"I don't know, but I know Tee over here does. Right Tee? You memba me."

Mark flicked his cigarette over the bench, and then spat on the ground. He then looked at Terrance and Will again. Terrance looked at him closely; he cocked his head to one side, squinted and finally recognized him.

"Oh…fucking Foster," he said with a smirk.

"Yea fuckin Foster." Mark said.

He reached in his jacket pocket and pulled out a .45 caliber. He raised it up and shot Will point blank in the chest. Terrance backed up quickly; he tried for his gun that was tucked in the waist of his pants at the small of his back.

"Don't even think about it," Mark said with a smile as he pointed the gat at Terrance.

"Shit!!" Terrance said.

Mark stepped up to him and pressed the gun against his fore head. He reached around back and pulled the gun out from his waist and tossed it in the bushes behind him.

"When yall Mutha fuckas pushed me down them train station steps, all I could think about was, man Mark cover your face. And when I look up all I see is you…" Mark rubbed his jaw line and stepped back.

"Take your shirt off."

"What??" Terrance asked.

"Take your jacket and shirt off!" he repeated slowly.

"Man fuck you!"

"Take you shit off! Now!!"Mark yelled.

As Terrance unbuttoned his leather jacket, Mark continued, "You bought your foot down, right on my nose…Shit, that hurted. I blacked out and when I woke up yall niggas was still kicking me."

Mark laughed out loud. Standing naked from the waist up, Terrance stared at Mark. Mark was laughing so hard, tears rolled down his cheeks.

"Crazy Mutha fucka," Terrance said.

Mark stopped.

"Ohhhhh I'm crazy? What's today Tee?" he asked but didn't wait for a response. "Two years ago today you killed my boy Saquan. I told em...but no one believed me...I told them tho..."

Mark squeezed the trigger. The bullet flew through the air and hit Terrance in the face. The impact of the bullet lifted him up off his feet and threw him back a few paces. Mark stood still for a minute, gun still pointed. He finally walked slowly over to Terrance and looked down.

"Oh shit son," he said out loud.

Terrance was sprawled out on his back with his right eye open but the entire left side of his face was gone.

"Where your face at?"

Mark stood and looked in amazement. Off in the distance he could hear police sirens, he dropped the gun at his feet and pulled a steak knife out of his other pocket. He straddled Terrance, sat on his stomach and began to carve his name in his chest. By the time the police reached him, he was just finishing up the letter K.

The killings made the morning papers with headlines such as, "BABIES KILLING BABIES." Or with stories that read,"17 year old Terrance Romain was shot in the face by Mark Anderson, 16. Police say the murder stems from an on going territorial gang war between Vector houses and neighboring Foster..."

Two years after the Romain's front door was shot down and their seven-year-old daughter was rushed to the hospital with a gunshot wound to the shoulder, they buried their 17-year-old son. The death of Terrance drove a wedge between the already strained marriage of Reggie and Mary. After 6 more months of constant bickering, Mary suggested marriage counseling to Reggie, he in return suggested divorce. Six years after Jada lost her brother; there she stood wondering whether or not her father was going to come to her sweet 16-birthday party.

"Jay? You alright?" Monica asked while viewing her friend.

"Yea…I haven't spoken to my father in awhile, so I don't know…"

Cancer and Calvin drove down Thornwood and stopped directly across from 3210. Cancer made it his business to check on Mary and Jay and give them whatever they might need. He watched Jada as she stood there, deep in conversation with Monica. He couldn't help notice how much she had grown. He watched her run her fingers through her long black hair, watched her scoop it up then let it all drop back down to her shoulders. He looked her up and down, took notice of how big the sweatshirt she had on was and how tight the jeans were. He focused on her thighs and let out a low, "ummm."

"Who you looking at like that?" Calvin asked.

"Huh?"

"Oh Jay and Monie, yea them some pretty ass hoes."

Cancer smacked Calvin up side the back of his head.

"Why you do that?"

"How you gonna call Jay a hoe? Who she sleeping with? How many ma fuckas? Huh? You don't know do you? Don't ever let me hear you speak no ill shit bout her again."

"Damn son! Aight yo, you got it," Calvin said while rubbing the back of his head.

Cancer leaned on the horn and looked in the direction of both girls. They both looked over and waved.

"You gonna invite Cancer?" Monica asked.

"I doubt he would wanna come. He's what? 23? But if he wanna come he can."

"You know he does," Monica said with a smile. "He is sweating you hard."

Jada just looked at her friend and rolled her eyes.

"Jay and Cancer sitting in a tree…" she began to sing.

"Alright now you need to chill…he's like an older brother Monie, you know that. He was Terry's best friend, he used to sleep over my house, and he's known me since I was little."

"Well you ain't so little no more Jay. And I bet he would love to come sleep over at your house again, just like the old days," Monica said with a laugh.

"Night Monie, you getting on my nerves," Jada said while stepping back into the house.

"Alright, alright, I'm a chill. See you tomorrow gurl."

"Ok, don't forget, jeans with holes and a turtleneck. Oh and please please call me when you get in your house. Mommy will worry half to death if you don't"

Both girls said their goodbyes and Jay closed the door. Cancer pulled off once she did.

ROMELO

"2, 4, 6, 8 what cha gonna do? 2,4,6,8 Lincoln's gonna annihilate you!"Jada yelled along with the rest of the cheerleading squad.

"Don't get mad, don't get sad. Didn't they tell yall Lincoln was bad!!"

Jada jumped out in front of the rest of the crowd and lead them in a cheer that involved her doing a split at the end. The crowd roared, this got Romelo's attention. His team was gathered in a huddle and usually Ro didn't pay attention to the crowd at away games but for some reason he looked over a teammates shoulder and saw what the commotion was all about. Rob Base and D.J. E-Z Roc's "It takes two" was blasting, most of the home crowd were on their feet and the cheerleaders were breaking down a dance routine that combined the running man, a little pop locking and the bump. Ro couldn't take his eyes off of the one in the front. Jada did the bump with a cheerleader next to her; she held one yellow pom-pom in her left hand and a red pom-pom in her right. Ro watched her intently; he liked the way her hair was pulled up into a high ponytail. He watched the smile on her face grow brighter with every step she made. He glanced at her thighs that were somewhat revealed thanks to the short red&white cheerleader skirt. When the girls stopped pop locking they yelled," here's a blast from the past. Now watch Lincoln kick they…" They all held up their pointer fingers, swiveled their hips and pointed to their backsides. The crowd roared, even Ro smiled.

"Jones!" coach yelled.

"Yea coach."

"You payin attention to me or to the skirts ova there?"

"To you coach Calhoun, always. Don't worry I got chu. And coach?"

"What?" he asked.

"Chill out, it's only a pre-season game." Ro smiled at Coach Calhoun and ran onto the court. He looked for the pretty cheerleader he was admiring a few minutes ago and found her standing behind the player's bench talking to another girl. He walked past them and both his and Jada's eyes locked. He smiled at her, she smiled back. Romelo was lost in her eyes; he could not believe how beautiful she was. He wanted to talk to her, ask her her name, hold her hand, take her to a movie, spend time with her, just be in her presence. For a second he closed his eyes and pictured his lips on hers, imagined how soft they must feel. Ro was jarred from his fantasy by a blow to the back of his right shoulder. He turned to find Calvin retrieving the basketball that he had just thrown at him.

"D up muthafucka. You come to play ball or what?" Calvin asked with a smirk on his face.

Romelo tucked his shirt in his shorts and pulled on the drawstrings.

"I came to beat your ass," he said.

The announcer thanked the crowd for coming, announced both teams, their coaches, and reminded the crowd that this was just a game. Romelo held the position of shooting guard. After getting first possession of the ball, he drove to the court and made eye contact with Jada again. She stood behind the player's bench watching him with a confused look on her face. Tre stole the ball from his man and dished a no look pass to Ro, who immediately squared up for a three. SWISHHH.

The crowd booed but his teammates hollered. He was feeling in the zone tonight. Not because he wanted to kick Lincoln's ass but because he knew his future wife was watching him. And with that thought, Ro laughed out loud.

"What the fuck is wrong with me?" he asked himself.

Lincoln's center missed his shot and A.J. rebounded the ball, bought it up court and passed it to Ro. Calvin quickly left his man and decided to play Ro on this possession.

He stepped in front of Ro and eyed him.

"What nigga?"Calvin asked.

Romelo smiled at him and dribbled to his left, he started to run towards the basked but then pulled up for a shot instead. He faked and this got Calvin off his feet, he was called for the foul. Again the crowd booed. Ro stepped to the free throw line and looked over at Jada. He bounced the ball three times, bent his knees, looked at the basket and shot the ball.

"And he makes the first one..." the public announcer said.

Ro looked over to Jada and winked, she smiled. Calvin caught this exchange and immediately scanned the crowd for Cancer. He knew Cancer said he was coming to the game tonight to watch Truman get their Asses beat. Ro sunk the second free throw, which gave him seven points and made Lincolns coach call for a time out. During the time out huddle, Ro walked to the table to get a cup of water. He watched Lincoln's cheerleaders but really he only had eyes for one. What is her name he wondered. Just then the girl who had been talking with her walked up to him and smiled.

"Hi."

"Hi," he said back.

"My name is Monica."

"Hi Monica. Ummm is that your friend over there?" he asked while looking in Jada's direction.

"Yea."

"What's her name?" he asked a little too excitedly.

"That's my home girl Jada."

"Jada," he whispered.

He watched Jada walk off the court, giving high fives to the other cheerleaders. He loved her smile, the way her lips curled, the shine they had to them. Lip gloss maybe, he thought. He also loved the fullness of them, how the bottom one looked slightly larger then the top. Her butter pecan complexion looked flawless to him. Ro couldn't stop staring.

"Jones!" Coach yelled again.

"Damn," he said. "Do me a favor Monica; tell Jada this next basket is for her."

"Okay," Monica said with a huge smile. She ran over to her friend screaming. Coach Calhoun walked up to Ro and smacked him on the back of the head.

"Did you hear what I said? Did you hear the whistle? Did you hear anything? What's wrong with you Jones?"

Romelo looked over at Jada then back to his coach. He grabbed the black Marker that was sticking out of coach's front shirt pocket. He then bent and scribbled the letter J on both his sneakers.

"What's wrong with me coach? I dunno...I think im in love."

Ro gave coach back the marker, patted him on the back and ran back onto the court with a smile.

"Oh lord, nuthin worse then a baller in love," Coach mumbled to himself.

"You aight?" Butta asked while giving Ro the ball.

"Yea I'm cool."

"Nature and Rugged here. Just saw them come in."

Ro looked in the direction Butta was looking. He found Nature and Rugged talking to Coach.

"Let's make this a pretty one son." He said after throwing the ball back to Butta. The ball was imbounded and Butta bought it up court. He motioned to A.J. to set a pick. A.J. stepped up and stopped Lincoln's point guard right in his tracks. Ro lost his man and made a dash to the basket, reading Ro's eyes, Butta threw the ball high towards the basket. Calvin left his man and ran towards Ro. As Ro went up for the alley-oop, Calvin pushed him hard. Causing Ro to crash down to the ground. The ref's whistle blew and the audience grew quiet. Romelo lay on the court quietly, while his teammates surrounded him.

"Ro? You all right?" asked A.J.

"Shake it off nigga," said Butta.

Ro opened his eyes and sat up slowly. Some audience members began to clap. The ref blew his whistle and yelled;" flagrant foul!"

Ro was helped to his feet; he looked around and saw Nature being held back by Coach Calhoun. The ref blew his whistle again and Calvin was hit with a technical this time. As Ro walked to the free throw line, Calvin was led off the court cursing and yelling the whole time. He had a short discussion with his coach and kicked over a chair. That action got him thrown out of the game.

Ro stood at the free throw line and bounced the ball three times, as he bent at the knees he felt a stabbing pain in his lower back. He grimaced in pain and shot the ball. He looked over at Jada, who was clapping for him, and winked at her. After making both shots, Coach Calhoun called a time out.

"Jones, you okay?"

"Yea, I'm aight."

"Damn, son tried to end you right there," Rugged said while giving up some dap.

"Bitch mad cause his skills ain't up to parr," Nature said.

"That's alright, let him hate if he want too. Just makes his ass look stupid," Ro said while giving Nature a hug and some dap.

"Ain't nuthin but Vector up in here, as usual. That's why we came. Member when we used to play here at Lincoln Rugged?"

"Hells yea, a fight broke out every time. Somebody was leaving with a broken arm, cracked skull, something," Rugged said with a laugh.

Rugged's pager interrupted the conversation.

"Yo son that's us, this the number I've been waiting for. We gotta roll out."

"Ro, take my keys, drive Trevor, A.J. and Butta home. Page me soon as you get in," Nature said while giving his car keys to Romelo.

"And don't act a fool, you ain't got no license and I'm not tryna make a trip to central booking tonight."

Rugged reached in his pocket and passed Ro a twenty-dollar bill.

"Get chall something to eat…wait hole up…I know them ain't the new kicks I just bought you?"

All three looked down.

"Yea, they are."

"What you do? Draw on em?"

"Nawww, that's the letter J," Ro said with a smile.

Ro looked in the direction of Jada, Nature and Rugged followed his stare.

"Ohhh, some chick?" Rugged smiled at Ro and gave him a pound.

"Aight we out."

"What I say nigga?" Nature asked.

"Go straight home and page you."

"Stop treating him like a baby. Little man got dirt under his nails just like you," Rugged said while pushing Nature towards the exit.

Truman high beat Lincoln with a score of 79-63 that night.

Calvin sat in the locker room listening and brooding. Every time he heard the announcer mention Ro by name or by jersey number, he got even more pissed. He didn't appreciate being thrown out of the game but what was even worse, he thought, was the looks Jada and Romelo had exchanged.

"Bitches from Vector don't fuck with niggas from Foster. Wait till Cancer finds out," he said aloud.

"Wait till Cancer finds out what?" Cancer asked while walking in the locker room with Rayson and Tariq.

"What chu doin in here talking to yourself? I see yall lost...again and where's Jada?"

"That's what I was talking bout. I don't know where she is but that nigga Ro was tryna push up on her all night."

"For real?" Cancer asked.

"Hell yea...and...and Nature and Rugged rolled thru tryna start some shit also. I wasn't having it tho. That's why they kicked me out da game."

"Nature and Rugged? Say word..." Cancer automatically began rubbing on the gun that was tucked in his belt, the one he never left home without.

"Aight then, Lata."

Cancer walked out the locker room in search of Jada.

After having listened to a disciplinary speech from Coach, Ro didn't even shower; he grabbed his knapsack and ran back to the gym. A few people stood around talking, but no Jada in sight. AJ, Tre and Butta caught up with him.

"Good game yo," Tre said.

"You ready to bounce?" Butta asked.

"Where is she?" Ro asked to no one in particular.

"Who?"

"The cheerleader...the fine one, her name is Jada."

"Which one? Cause they all was fine," A.J. said while holding his fist out for some dap that no one bothered to give him.

"Jada, she had her hair pulled up in a ponytail, pretty smile, she was in the middle…"

"Ooohhh yea, the fineeee one. I don't know where she went tho. Probably went home, most of dem chicks are from Vector anyway," Tre said while sucking his teeth.

"Naw, I don't think so, I've never seen her before," said Ro.

"And so what if she is? Shit let me catch a fine honey from Vector. Dem niggas come round our way and…"

"Ahh shit, here he go. Please do not get Butta started," said Trevor.

"It's true though," Butta said in defense.

"Yea it is, but ummmm Butta you gots a girl."

"And?" Butta replied. They all laughed out loud.

"Romeo over here needs to loosen up his grip and let some of us ugly niggas get one of his."

"I ain't got no girl," Romeo said.

"And who you calling ugly?" Tre asked.

"You may not claim them but they sure do claim yo ass," A.J. replied.

"Where's Romeo? Give Romeo my numba, tell Romeo I said hi…" Butta said while doing his best trying to sound like a girl.

"Whateva nigga," Ro said with a laugh.

"Yo let's go…I'm hungry." Trevor said.

They all began to walk towards the gym exit.

"Oh dang, I forgot I gots the whip yall," Ro said while holding up the car keys.

"Aight!! Were we going?" Butta asked.

"KFC," said A.J.

"Bet!" replied Butta.

"I don't want any KFC."

"Well we all do nigga, so you is out voted," A.J. said.

"You not scared are you? Cause that's Vector territory?" Butta asked.

"No. We in Vector territory now aint we? Do I look like I'm scared?"

"Well ahhh…" A.J. said laughing.

"Whateva…I got the keys so if yall want KFC yall gonna hafta walk. But, if yall going to Mickey Dee's, with me, then lets go. If not well umm seeeeeee ya!!"

"That's alright dawg. I wanna check out these Vector chicks anyway. So I'm walking, let's go A.J." Butta said.

"And Tre?" Ro asked while holding the keys up to Trevor's face.

"Yo son, I can't even front. I want some greasy, nasty, oily…you know the type where da oil be dripping down your chin, type chicken." Tre said.

"Only your moms makes chicken like dat, not KFC."

"Ohhhhh, momma jokes?" Tre asked.

"Your moms so dumb, I told her to take da four train and she took da two train twice." Butta said while laughing.

"Let's get off mommas son. Aiight, lets get off mommas, I just got off yours." Tre said.

"Aight forget chall," Ro exchanged pounds with all three and exited the gym.

"Which way?" A.J. asked.

"Let's go out the back way, that's gonna let us out facing the bridge. We just cross ova The Bridge and walk down…" Tre said.

"Naw, we can cut threw Secore houses and come up the back way," Butta said.

"Whatever yo, let's just get there. I'm hungry as a fuck," A.J. said while buttoning his jacket. They exited Lincoln from the back and began to walk towards the over street bridge. When they came to Baychester Avenue, things livened up a little. Despite the chilly September night cars crowded the streets and people were gathered either outside the corner bodega or the Baychester Ave. train station. Butta spotted some girls leaning against a parked car. He pulled the black band that held all his dreads in place off his head and let his dreads hang loose.

"Dang, look at honey ova there" he said to A.J. and Tre.

"Which one?" A.J. asked.

"The one with the beige boots on."

The girls eyed them as they passed; Butta smiled and motioned for her to come to him. The one with the beige boots told him to come to her instead.

"Hold up yall, let me see what she talking bout."

He walked over to the small crowd and introduced himself.

"Damn, I wish he come on," A.J. said while looking in Butta's direction. Butta had stepped to the side and was no doubt charming the girl in the beige boots because she was all smiles.

"I want a cigarette," Tre said.

"Since when you smoke?" asked A.J.

"Since now nigga, damn! You sounding like my grandmother."

"Whateva yo, I just wanna get out of here…don't feel right. I still aint do my homework. Aye yo, you got me on the chicken right?"

"Hole up dog. You do homework?"

"How else am I supposed to graduate? You need to do some."

"Naw, that's what my girl is for. And what chu mean do I got you on the chicken?"

"I'm broke man…you got me?"

Trevor just sucked his teeth and looked in Butta's direction.

"Aye any of yall got a pen?" Butta yelled.

Both A.J. and Trevor shook their heads no. Butta walked up to them with beige boots in tow, and made introductions.

"Octavia, this is my nigg Tre and my other nigg A.J. Yall this is Octavia."

"What up," said Tre.

"How you doing?" asked A.J.

"Hi," she replied.

"Yo, let's walk down to KFC; I'm sure I could get a pen from inside of there."

After standing on line and ordering their chicken, they all decided to eat on the walk back home to Foster.

At the same time Calvin and his crew were headed back to Vector but decided to stop at the only bodega that was open at this time. A beer run was what they had in mind and this particular bodega never asked them for I'd. As Calvin stopped to show love to some of his peeps on the ave. he spotted Butta standing outside KFC chattin up Octavia.

"Yo, tell me I'm buggin out," he said to no one in particular.

"I know that's not dem niggas from Foster down there?"

The word Foster automatically drew a small crowd that stood next to Calvin and all heads turned to see if he was buggin out or not.

"Yea that's them," Rayson said.

"Oohhh I hope dat nigga Ro is wit em. Yo yall let's go this way, meet these fools head on," Calvin said with a smile. He, Rayson and a couple others, headed back down Baychester and then headed towards Mark Towers houses. Butta said goodnight to Octavia and promised to call her tomorrow.

"Gimmie my chicken," he said to A.J.

"She a cutie, said she likes my dreads and shit."

They passed the Baychester Motel and made a left. At the bottom of the hill stood Calvin and his crew.

"Who dat?" A.J. asked.

"Damn, that's dat nigga Calvin and Rayson," Butta replied.

All three slowed their pace. Calvin stood there screw facing them.

"How many your see?" Trevor asked. All three made a mental count.

"Six," whispered A.J.

"No, seven...there's one leaning against the car," Butta said.

"Shit...we should have gone with Ro."

"Chill A.J. Aiight yall it's like this. There are only 3 of us, 7 of them. If they tryna do this physically what we gonna do?" Butta asked.

A.J. made a whimpering sound; both Tre and Butta looked at him.

"What if they packing? I know Calvin packing," A.J. said.

"Yo yall we gonna hafta run, fuck it, split up."

They had stopped walking at this point and were just standing still.

"What they doin?" Rayson asked.

"Them niggas are shook. I don't see Romelo though."

A non-appearance of Romelo seemed to piss Calvin off even more then he had already been. He started to get impatient.

"Yo yall let's go," he said.

They began walking towards A.J. Trevor and Butta.

"Shit, here they come"

Calvin stuck his tongue out at Butta revealing a razor that sat right smack dab in the middle of it.

"Yea, they mean harm. I'm headed towards the bridge," Butta said.

"K, I'm going left...A.J. head right, that's the quickest way," Tre whispered.

"FOOOOSSSSSSSSTERRRRRR!!!" Calvin sang out.

"COME OUT AND PLAAAAYYYYY YAAAYYY!"

With his eyes glued to Calvin, Trevor whispered;" One...two..."

But before he could get to 3, A.J. took off. He ran in the direction Butta was supposed to take.

"Shit! Run Butta!" Trevor yelled.

"Get them niggas!" Calvin hollered.

Butta and Trevor ran back past the motel and under the train tracks.

"Split up!" Butta insisted.

"Go that way, meet me at the back handball courts, behind H building. If they catch you just drop and cover your face!"

Both Trevor and Butta ran as if their lives depended on it, and as far as they knew, it did. A.J. made it to the top of the bridge, he could hear footsteps behind him, and he knew they were catching up to him.

"Keep running," he told himself over and over again. "Don't stop…keep running."

He ran across the bridge, it had never seemed as long as it did to him now. His left side was beginning to give off pain. Tears welled up in his eyes and clouded his vision. A.J. felt as if he was going to throw up at any minute.

"Where you going mutha fucka?" someone yelled at him.

He was getting ready to descend down the steep bridge steps. "Soon I will be in Foster," he thought. "Keep running!" he cried out to himself.

He turned to see how far behind they were from him and suddenly lost his footing at the tip of the bridge steps. A.J. tumbled down; half way down his knap sack got caught on a piece of the wire link fence that was sticking out. His right arm was pulled up and over his head. A.J. screamed out in pain. This slowed his fall and A.J. just seemed to skid down the remaining three or four steps. Calvin and two others caught up to him, they stood over him laughing.

"Damn, you bust your ass!" Calvin yelled. They hopped and hollered and stomped their feet.

"Woooo, that was some funny shit. Get up ass!"

A.J. struggled to get to his feet, he felt pain all over, and knew he had to be bleeding from at least two different places. Calvin grabbed him by the shoulders and pushed him against the fence.

"Nice jacket...dang you fucked up the sleeve; ripped it. Oh well, I'll take it anyway."

He snapped open the buttons on A.J.'s red New York Yankee's jacket and pulled it off of him.

"Here hold that," he said while tossing the jacket to one of his homeboys.

"Where your boy Romelo at?" he asked.

A.J. didn't answer, to him this wasn't even happening, he saw Calvin's lips moving but for the life of him, he couldn't make out what he was saying.

"Oh you gonna play dumb? Alright...I was gonna let you walk but you want it this way huh?"

He held his hand under his chin and spit the razor out. When A.J. saw the razor his stomach knotted up. He tried to hold it in but couldn't. He threw up the KFC he had eaten earlier, with most of it landing on Calvin's boots.

"Oh hell no!" Calvin yelled.

And with one quick flick of his wrist, he slashed A.J. across his left cheek. Blood flowed like water. A.J. felt hotness on his face and put his right hand up to his cheek. When he saw all the blood on his hand he began to sink down to the ground.

"Catch him," Calvin instructed.

The other two held him up while Calvin slashed at his other cheek. Everything became a blur to A.J. at that point. He didn't even feel any more pain. All he could focus on was off in the distance, just past Calvin's shoulder. He could see Foster houses, A.J. smiled.

JADA

Jada had begged her mother for two days straight to let her cheer at the Lincoln-Truman pre season game.

"Mommy I'm one of the head cheerleaders this year. I hafta be there…" she moaned.

Mary finally gave in but under the conditions that Monica goes with her and Cancer drive them both there and back.

"Bet!" Jada said excitedly. She ran to her room and called Monica and of course Monica was down to go anywhere that required the presence of boys. She then paged Cancer; he called her back before she could put the receiver back on its cradle, or so it seemed to Jada.

"Give me 15," he said.

Jada sat down on her bed and began brushing her shoulder length black hair. She was glad her mother had decided to let her go. That was a relief; her mother was starting to let her do some things by herself. Jada remembered how last year, her mother wouldn't let her cheer at away games. "To dangerous," she would say. Jada pulled her hair back into a tight ponytail. She remembered how there was a time her mother wouldn't even let her go shopping for a pair of sneakers by herself. Cancer's car horn pulled Jada away from her thought process. As she left her bedroom she almost bumped into her mother who was headed to get her.

"Cancer's here."

"I know, I heard the horn."

"I wish they wouldn't make these skirts so short," her mother said while trying to pull Jada's cheerleading skirt down.

"Shows off my sexy thighs," Jada said with a giggle.

"No one needs to see your sexy thighs," her mother retorted.

They both walked downstairs together hand in hand. Mary opened the front door and both she and Jay waved to Cancer's cream-colored Acura.

"Ok mommy, see you later."

Oh wait…here." Her mother gave her a sweater.

"In case the gym is too chilly."

Jada took the sweater from her mother and leaned in and gave her a kiss on her cheek.

"I love you mommy, and please don't worry…I'm gonna be okay. I got big brother Cancer looking out for me."

"I know baby, you know I can't help but worry."

"I know but don't…kay?"

"Ok," her mother said almost reluctantly.

Jada ran to Cancer's car and opened the passenger door; the sounds of The Brand Nubians filled the air.

"Hey, what's up?" Jada yelled, trying to out do Grand Puba.

"Sup Jay."

Cancer turned down the volume and then looked at Jada.

"What?" she asked.

"Nuthin...they make them skirts short don't they?"

"Ewwww, you sound just like my mother."

Cancer could relate to Mary, he wanted to tell Jada to go back in the house and put on some pants, some really huge, baggy pants. But she would probably look just as sexy in them too, he imagined. The thought of other guys having these same thoughts of Jay burned Calvin up.

"Thanks for coming to get me," she said.

"No problem...listen Jay if I don't make it back to Lincoln in time, you and Monica wait right out front. Im a send someone else to scoop yall. But that's only if I don't make it back on time okay?"

"Ok, that's cool."

They stopped to get Monica, and then headed for Lincoln high. For the whole ride Monica talked non-stop about this guy in her science class or that guy in her gym class. Calvin even turned up the volume but that didn't stop her. He was glad Jay didn't talk like that, he had never heard her even mention a boys name, at least not in his presence. He parked the car and looked over at her.

"Memba what I said."

"Yea, we will wait right here."

"Oh dang, I forgot to tell yall, my moms is gonna come get me afterwards, we gonna go get some food. You can ride wit us Jay," Monica said while checking out some guys standing outside the gym entrance.

"Naw, she cool...I'm a come git her," Cancer said.

From the back seat, Monica pulled on Jada's ponytail. When Jay turned to look at her, Monica gave her a,' see I told you he like you' look.

"Anyway," Jada said while rolling her eyes at her friend.

Monica got out the car and started for the gym entrance.

"Thanks again Cancer. Oh, listen my birthday is in a few days..."

"Yea, I know," he interrupted.

"Kay, well...I'm having a party and you could come if you want too. I know the crowd might be too young for you..."

"Aight, no doubt. I'm there. Where at?"

"The community center."

"Say word, moms is letting you have it at the center? She probably hiring security for the joint," he said laughing.

"I know right? Don't give her any ideas please. Ok let me go, see you in a little while."

"Yea, right here," Cancer, reminded.

Jada jumped out of the car and caught up with Monica. They could hear, "...one for all, Brand Nubians..." blasting from his car as he pulled out of the school parking lot.

At game time, Jada was happy to learn that all of the squad had practiced her new routine and was ready to do it tonight. It wasn't a full house but the crowd was big enough for her. She jumped out front and led them in the first cheer, the crowd loved it. Jada ran off the court all smiles. Monica gave her a high five and a hug.

"You worked it gurl!!" she yelled.

"Dang Jay who is that checking you out?" Monica asked while looking in Romelo's direction.

Jada turned to see who it was that Monica was talking about and saw him. A tall, fine, brown skinned guy who was staring right back at her. He then smiled at her and Jada felt like she might melt. She couldn't take her eyes off of him, his caramel skin looked silky smooth to her. It was all that she could do to keep herself from running onto the court and talking to him. She wanted to hear his voice, learn his name, tell him hers then listen to him say it over and over and over again. She wanted to run her fingers over the waves in his hair or play with the dimples in his cheeks she saw every time he smiled.

"Hold up!" Monica yelled.

"Did you see Calvin? He threw the ball at cutie while he was checking you out."

"Monie? Who is that?" Jada asked, almost in a whisper.

"I don't know Jay, I've never seen him before. But he is on the other team so maybe he's from Foster."

"Foster?" Jay asked.

She could not tear her eyes away from him. Every time their eyes met, she felt funny. Some sort of feeling in her stomach, this confused her. As Romelo made his first two points he ran up the court and glanced at her. Confusion was written all over her face.

"Monie?"

"What's up Jay?"

"Do me a favor; find out his name for me and where he's from."

"Ok, bet! Wait till a time out or something."

Jada watched him walk up court, she watched his legs, they seemed bowed. She even glanced at his butt and became immediately embarrassed.

"He is definitely a cutie Jay, so is number 5 and point guard number 26. Wait, here go Calvin again, he caused a time out."

Jada forced herself to get on the court with the rest of the cheerleaders during the time out. It was hard for her to focus on the cheers knowing Monica was standing over there talking to him. She glanced in their direction and they were both looking at her. There goes that feeling in her stomach again. She hoped no one noticed her mess up that last routine.

"Go Lincoln!" they all yelled and ran off the court. "Play it off girl...stop staring," she told herself as she walked back to the bench. But it was no use, every time she looked at him; he was smiling back at her. Jay felt like they were the only two people in the gym and she wanted so bad to run into his arms.

"Ooooohhh!" Monica ran to her screaming.

"What?" Jay asked nervously.

"Ok...ok, he said...check this out, he said his name is Romelo."

"Romelo?" Jay asked.

"Yep, isn't that cute? Sounds like Romeo."

"He can be my Romeo," Jay whispered.

"Oh and Jay, he asked me your name and said to tell you that this next basket is for you girl!"

"Oh my God, really?"

Monica and Jada watched as Romelo ran down court and right when he jumped in the air, was hacked by Calvin. Jada watched in horror as Romelo crashed to the ground and yelled out in pain.

"Oh shit!" Monica said.

The crowd got quiet suddenly and watched as Romelo's teammates ran to his aide.

60

"Owww!" Monie said while looking at Jada.

"Jay! You are squeezing the mess out of my arm!"

Jada hadn't realized that she had a monster grip on her friends arm. She loosened up her grip and apologized.

"I have to go to him Monie," she said. "He's hurt…"

"Chill Jay, he gon be alright, look he's sitting up now."

Some of the crowd began to clap, as did Monie and Jay. Calvin was led off the court and due to his childish behavior was thrown out of the game. He walked past Jada and Monica, and while taking his jersey off he gave Jay an evil look. She returned his screw face with one of her owns. Monica booed him as he past.

"Boooo! That's why no one likes his ass. He always tryna start some shit. He stay in trouble…I can't stand him. And why did he look at you like that?"

"I don't know, forget Calvin," Jay said, eyes glued to #66, Romelo Jones.

Ro made the first basket and Jada clapped loudly. This caught the attention of some of her fellow cheerleaders.

"Which team you cheering for?" someone yelled out.

"I'm cheering for #66," She said to herself.

And it was as if he had read her mind, he turned to look at her and even winked. Jada had to sit down.

"What's wrong Jay?"

"I don't know Monie. I feel funny…it's…it's like there are little men inside my stomach, stomping around with steel boots on."

"Huh?" Monica asked confused.

"I don't know either Monie. I can't explain it but I only feel that way when he looks at me."

"Ohhh!" Monica said with a huge smile.

"You're in love!" Heyyyyy my girls in love!" she sang out.

"No Monica!" Jada was embarrassed. She grabbed Monica's arm and pulled her down onto the bench next to her.

"Owww! There you go diggin them nails in my arm again."

"Sorry, but ssshhh! I'm not in love. How can I be? Doesn't it work differently? I mean, aren't we supposed to meet, go out, go dancing maybe…share a kiss and then some where down the line…"

"Gurl please! This ain't television or some romance novel. You always got your head stuck in some sort of fairy tale. Haven't you heard of love at first site?" Monica asked.

"Love at first site," Jay repeated.

Monica looked at her friend and giggled.

With only 23 seconds left in the game, Truman high school was ready to count this one as a win. Lincoln was down by 16 points and most of the crowd was headed towards the exits. For the rest of the game, Jada had trouble concentrating on anything else but Romelo. She even silently cheered for him every time he scored. She hated that the game was over so quickly. Maybe she would never see him again, never get the chance to talk to him or worse yet, never get the chance to kiss him. That thought alone caused her heart some pain. She just knew after the game, he would come over to her, bend down, kiss her hand, and then whisk her away, leaving all the others in envy. But he didn't, he walked into the locker room with the rest of his team. Giving pounds and pats to each other, either to the back of the head or butt.

"Love at first site…yea right, I'm trippin," Jada said out loud.

"What?" the cheerleader next to her asked.

"Oh…nuthin. See you at practice." Jada said with a sad smile.

"Jay, I'm out. You sure you don't want to ride with moms and me? We are going to get some Burger King."

"Naw, I'm a wait out front for Cancer."

"Cancer would be pissed if he seen the way you was flirting with Romeo."

"I wasn't flirting Monie. And why would Cancer be pissed? He's not my man! Annddd he has a gurl, thank you."

"Ummmmm hmmm, tell him that. Wait speaking of Romeo, where is he?"

"I don't know, he left I guess." Jada said while gathering up her pompoms.

They both headed for the school exit. Monica then turned back to face the somewhat empty gym and yelled out, "Oh Romeo, Romeo, where for art thou Romeo?"

Both girls broke out into laughter.

"You so silly Monie," Jay said while laughing.

They walked out of the gym, arms around each other yelling, "deny thy father and refuse thy name."

Monica's mother was already outside waiting on her. She leaned on the horn once she spotted both girls.

"Alright mom! I'm coming! You sure?" she asked Jada while pointing to the car.

"I'm sure, it's cool. Go head and call me when yall get back."

"Ok," Monica hugged her, and ran to her mother's car.

Jada put the sweater on that her mother had given her. She was pissed at herself for not bringing a change of clothes. At least a pair of jeans or something she thought.

She checked the time on her Winnie the Pooh watch; it read 8:28 pm.

"Alright Cancer, let's go. Its getting cold out here," she said aloud. A couple of cars drove by honking their horns at her but Jada ignored them.

Romelo drove Nature's used, beat up Cadillac out of the parking lot and swung around to the front of Lincoln. He was hoping to catch Butta and them because he forgot to mention the $20.00 Rugged had given him. He couldn't believe his eyes when he saw her, Jada standing alone outside the gym. He looked around and hoped that she wasn't waiting for her boyfriend. He watched as she rocked back and forth and pulled her sweater tight around her. "Damn, she's so fine" he thought.

Jada had seen the sky blue caddy pull up. She couldn't make out who was behind the wheel but it had to be some old pervert, the way he was creeping along, she thought. She moved into a more lit area and looked at her watch again. She glanced at the beat up caddy and wished whoever it was would just leave. Then the car started moving in her direction. Jada looked around nervously and decided to go back into the school and page Cancer with a 911. When she started to walk back, she could hear the window being let down and some one call her name.

"Hey Jada?"

She turned to see who it was that knew her and her eyes lit up when she recognized who it was. Play it cool, she reminded herself.

"Hey," was her reply.

"Do you need a ride?" Romelo asked.

Jada looked at her watch again, then up and down the street, she wanted to run to the car and jump in, but she was playing it cool, so she thought.

"I don't know you, and I don't get into cars with strangers."

Ro got out of the car and walked around front of it. Jada watched him; he still had his white Truman basketball shorts on but had put a huge green polo hoodie on over his jersey. He walked up to her and extended his hand.

"Hi, I'm Romelo Jones. Most of my friends call me Ro."

Jada looked down at his hand and then back up at him.

"I don't bite," he said with a smile.

"Oh my God," she thought. "Look at that smile."

She put her hand in his and he squeezed it.

"I'm Jada…Jada Romain. And most of my friends call me Jay."

Just the touch of his hand made her feel warm inside. It was as if neither one wanted to let go of the others hand. Finally Jay pulled hers away. The sounds of thunder were heard above and both looked up to the sky. Romelo immediately walked to the car and opened the passenger side door.

"Please Jada, let me drive you home fore it starts raining. I promise to keep both hands on the wheel. Unless you're waiting for your boyfriend then I can understand," he said while hopping and praying she would say that she didn't have one.

"No, I'm not waiting for my boyfriend because I don't have one."

"Yes!"

"Huh?" she asked.

"Nuthin, come on then Jada Romain."

Jay walked to the car and got in, she couldn't believe this, she had never done anything like this before. But she didn't feel scared or like she was putting herself in harms way. As a matter of fact, it felt all too natural to her; she did however wonder what her mothers reaction would be if she knew where she was at this very moment.

Ro walked around to the driver's side and got in.

"Don't blow this yo," he said to himself.

He started the engine and then looked over at Jada. She was looking at him with a funny expression on her face.

"What? Do I stink? I mean I have been playing ball…"

"No…it's just that I don't…"

"I'm not a psycho, trust. And look both hands are on the wheel."

Jada laughed. "Good game Romelo Jones," she said.

"Oh no doubt. I saw you checkin me out."

"I was not checking you out. I was watching, you know…all the players."

"Umm hmm ok. So I guess you go to Lincoln huh?"

"Yep."

"Okay. So which way am I going?"

"Go straight. You go to Truman?"

"Yeah," he answered.

"I've never seen you before though. You new to the area or something?" Ro asked while stopping at a red light.

"Nope, lived here my whole life, I didn't cheer that much last year."

In the sky lightening was doing a dance while thunder banged. Finally the rain began to pour. Ro switched on the window shield wipers and they made a squeaky noise. Jada laughed.

"Hey don't laugh, this is my older brother's baby. He claims he's gonna hook it up one day."

"Oh ok, so this is not your car?"

"Hell no!" They both laughed out loud.

"You can make a right at the next corner," she instructed.

Ro was so consumed by Jada's presence that he didn't notice where he was until now. He glanced at the street sign and realized he was in Vector Houses. Jada was asking him something but he didn't hear. He was getting flash backs of that night he sat between Rugged and Saquan as they were riding down this very same street. Then his thoughts drifted to Saquan.

Romelo was jarred from his thinking when he felt Jada's hand on his arm.

"You ok?" she asked.

"Yea, I'm cool. I didn't realize that you lived in Vector."

"Yea...and I'm guessing since you play for Truman you live in Foster?"

"Yea," he said.

They rode in silence for a few minutes, each preoccupied with thoughts of the whole Foster/Vector war. Finally Jada said; "you can let me out here if you want."

"Why? Is this your house"?

"No, but..."

"Naw, I'm a take you to your front door. It's pouring out here."

"Kay, well this next block on the corner is me."

Romelo read the street sign, Thornwood. His chest felt tight and he started to break out in a sweat as he made a left at the corner.

"Right here is cool," Jay said.

Romelo didn't want to look to his right and read the house number, he already knew. Jada couldn't understand why he seemed quiet all of a sudden. She figured it had to do with her living here in Vector. They both sat in silence for a minute, staring out at the rain as it beat on the car window.

"So Romelo Jones, do you have a girlfriend?" Jada asked.

"Naw...I'm single," he said with a smile.

Again, silence.

Ro stared straight ahead, not wanting to believe where he now sat.

Jada finally interrupted the silence with; "It turned out to be a nasty night."

Romelo looked at her. "No it didn't," he said.

She looked him in his eyes and felt those spike boots stomping around in her stomach again.

"Listen Jada I don't care about Vector and Foster. I want to see you again. Can I? Can I see you again?"

"Yea," she whispered.

"Yes? Did you say yes?" he asked excitedly.

Jada shook her head up and down. Romelo's face formed a huge smile.

"I don't know what it is Jay but I want to know you. Talk with you, be with you…"

Jada leaned closer to Romelo and put her fingers on his lips. He closed his eyes and felt his heart give in. She leaned even closer and kissed him. Jada felt as if she was going to melt. Their lips stayed pressed together for what seemed an eternity.

Across the street, sitting in his homeboy's black Ford Expedition, Cancer drew slowly on his Newport. He watched Romelo and Jada from behind tinted windows. He went to Lincoln to get her, he knew he was running a little late but he told her he might be didn't he? And she assured him she would wait if he were, didn't she? When he couldn't find her he went inside the school and learned that Romelo had been tryna push up on her. He couldn't understand why she wouldn't wait for him outside the school when she said that she would. And to make matters worse, here she sat, in Vector with someone from Foster. Cancer let these thoughts play over and over in his mind while he smoked the Newport down to its butt. He then tossed it out the car window. When Jay leaned in and kissed Ro, Cancer picked up the gun that sat on the seat beside him and pointed it in their direction.

"Fuckin pretty boy," he said aloud.

Romelo opened his eyes as Jada pulled her lips from his.

"I gotta go," she whispered.

"Don't…go with me. Let's just drive away. Forget Vector! Forget Foster! Let's just drive to ummmm…California."

"California?" she asked with a smile.

"You think this thing is gonna make it to California?"

Romelo laughed. "Doesn't hafta be Cali. We can go to Hawaii, Jamaica, anywhere you want to go. And if this thing breaks down then I will carry you on my back."

What Jada was feeling was indescribable. She was ready to go pack right now, didn't matter where they went as long as she was with him. She leaned into him again and pressed her lips on his. Romelo kissed her lips and thought that yes, this is the one for him. The motion lights outside of Jada's house came on and they both stopped kissing and looked to see who was there.

"My mom!" Jada said nervously, while she ducked down into the seat.

Ro watched Jada's mother stand inside the doorway of 3210. Flashbacks of that night filled his head again. He wanted to tell her that he stood outside her door eight years ago and shot bullets through it. But what if she hated him for it? What if she didn't want to ever see him again because of it? He couldn't bear that thought.

"Is she gone?" Jada asked.

"Yea."

Jada sat back up and looked towards her house.

"My mother worries a lot...cause my brother Terrence was killed two years ago. She's been talking about moving from here for the longest but says she can never seem to save up enough to do it. It's alright tho, because I'm going to be a high paid photographer one day and I'm gonna move her out of Vector."

Romelo thought about Jada's brother Terrance. He knew all about him dying in Vector Park, at the hands of Mark. He wondered if she knew all the foul shit Terrance had done while he was alive. He looked at her face, she seemed lost in thought.

"Boo...I'm serious. I want to go away one day and I want to take you with me. I'll play pro ball and you'll be a professional photographer. We can be happy and away from all this bullshit."

"Ok," Jay said.

"Okay?" Ro asked surprised.

"Yea...it seems ok. I want to be with you. This is crazy Ro but that's how I feel. I don't even know what your favorite color is or your favorite food but I do know I want to spend the rest of my life with you."

Hearing this come from Jada's mouth was the equivalent to making a buzzer basket during championships when both teams are tied, Romelo thought. Nothing else really mattered now. He knew what he had to do, finish high school, apply for college and get away from Foster, away with Jada.

"Red and French fries," he said.

"Huh?"

"My favorite color is red and my favorite food is French Fries."

"Ohhhhhhhhhh ok, now I know you," she said with a laugh.

"Do you believe in faith or destiny or any of that shit?" Ro asked.

"I don't know. I know I do believe in love at first site and I think the way something's turn out, that's the way it was meant to be..." Jada trailed off with a smile on her face.

"Well Romelo Jones, I hafta go for my mother calls the police, swat team, secret service, FBI, private investigators," she said while laughing.

"Ok Jada Jones," Ro said with a grin.

Jada opened the car door then turned to look at Ro.

"What did you just call me?" she asked.

"Nuthin."

He got out of the car, ran to the passenger side and opened the door for her. They walked hand in hand to her front door. Cancer had seen enough, he turned the key in the ignition and started the SUV. He pushed the window down button and turned the radio up high. As Cancer pulled out of the parking space he drove the car slowly past Ro and Jay. The loud music caused both of them to look in his direction. After he made eye contact with them both, he sped off.

"Who was that?" Ro asked, still looking in the direction the black Ford had driven off in.

"Looked like Cancer," Jay answered.

"Damn...I betta go."

"He was just looking for me. He probably pissed because he was supposed to drive me home."

"Wait, hol up…I thought you didn't have a man," Ro said tensely.

"I don't Romelo," Jada replied with a smile.

Her smile automatically made him feel like taking her into his arms and just holding her.

"Cancer is like a big brother to me…he used to hang real tight with Terrance."

Ro couldn't believe what he was hearing. For a second he thought he should just walk away from this girl because it just seemed like trouble. Jada squeezed his hand a little tighter and looked into his eyes.

"He's not my boyfriend Ro."

He looked back at her and knew right then that he could never walk away from her.

"Hey, why do they call him Cancer anyway?"

"I used to think because it was his zodiac sign. But Terrance gave him that name. They both tried smoking cigarettes, Terry didn't like it but Cancer did I guess. He smoked all the time and Terry would clown him and tell him one of these days he was going to die of cancer. Everyone just started calling him cancer ever since."

"Oh…Tomorrow Jay. I'm a see you tomorrow. When school lets out, meet me at the foot of the bridge, you know where it's at right?"

"The bridge that separates Vector from Foster?" she asked.

"Yea that one, meet me there."

"Okay Ro," she said with a smile.

Ro backed away from her, still holding her hand. He had to force himself to let go; he was practically pulling her to him.

"Bye," he said.

"Bye," Jada whispered.

Ro turned and walked towards the car.

"Jada Jones," she said.

"Huh?"

"I like how that sounds...Jada Jones."

Ro just looked at her for a second, and then walked towards her. Jay met him halfway and they fell into each other's arms. He held her tight while she looked up into his eyes and whispered, "I don't want to let go."

"Then don't."

Their lips met again and stayed locked until Ro noticed the front light come on inside 3210.

"I think your moms is coming."

Jada pulled herself away from him and gave him a sad look.

"Don't look like that...tomorrow Jada Jones."

Romelo kissed Jada on her cheek and then walked back to the car and got in. Jay stood there looking at him, while the rain poured down.

"Jada!" her mother called from the doorway. "Why are you standing there in the rain?"

Romelo pulled off and waved goodbye, Jay waved back at him.

"Who was that? Cancer? Why you so late?"

"I had to wait for Cancer," Jada said while walking into the house.

"Well go take those wet clothes off. How was the game?"

"It was...it was the best game I have ever been too mom," Jada said with a smile.

"Really? So Lincoln won huh"?

74

"Nope, they lost." Jada ran upstairs taking two steps at a time, leaving her mother standing there with nothing but confusion written all over her face. She got out of her wet uniform, put her thick white terry cloth bathrobe on and plopped down on her bed. She lay their looking at the ceiling, while thinking about Ro.

"Oh my God!" she said out loud.

She jumped up and ran to her phone. She dialed Monica's number.

"Hello?

"Gurl!! What's up?"

"Where da hell you been Jay? Your mother called here twice..."

"Monie let me tell you!"

Jada told Monica everything, how he is so polite, sexy, how she felt inside when they kissed. Monica's reaction was mostly, "What? You go gurl! For real? Or Oh my God! With a few screams in between. After talking to Monica for almost an hour and describing in detail what she was going to wear to school tomorrow, Jada finally hung up. She showered, put on her Winnie the Pooh pj's and fell asleep to the thoughts of Romelo Jones.

*****

ROMELO

Romelo drove all the way to Foster on cloud nine. He entered apartment 5e and found Rugged and Nae Nae sitting at the kitchen table.

"Sup yall," he said with a grin.

Rugged and Nae Nae exchanged glances with each other then looked back at Ro. He went into the kitchen and gave Rugged some dap.

"What up?" Rugged asked.

Ro then leaned over and gave Nae Nae a forehead kiss and rubbed her stomach.

"Didn't I tell you not to do that?" she asked in disgust.

"My bad…dang what's wrong wit chall? Nigga like me feeling gooood!"

Ro went to the refrigerator and got himself two bananas and an orange.

"Nae Nae? You was at the game?" he asked in between bites of his banana.

"You know I was. I go to everyone."

"True. You seen son try to take me down?"

"Yea, Calvin is a fucking punk."

Romelo laughed, "Its aight," he said.

Rugged took the blunt he had behind his ear, put it in his mouth and lit it.

"I told you not to smoke that stuff around me Rug," Nae Nae said.

"Sorry…I'm stressed shit! You don't want?" he asked Nae Nae. She just shot him an evil look.

"Ro? You?" he asked.

"Naw, I'm cool."

"Well I'm bout to take this to the head, Nae Nae when Nature get back call me. I'm a be in the room," Rugged said while leaving the kitchen.

"Where Nature at?" Ro asked Nae Nae.

She didn't answer him; in fact she avoided eye contact with Romelo altogether. But Ro didn't even notice, he was still on a natural high after chillin with Jada. He looked at his older sister.

"Nae?"

"Yea," she answered.

"How you know you was in love with Rugged? I mean…what did you feel?"

"Huh? Why you asking me that?"

"I just wanna know," he said while shrugging his shoulders.

"Well…we were on the train platform one night right? And it was mad cold outside. It was like two in the morning and we were on the A train platform in Queens, the outside one. I was freezing and shit. Rugged said to me, in this real sweet voice, not the rugged one yall hear. He said,' Tanaesha, come here." I walked over to him and he took his coat off and put it on me. As cold as it was, he stood there on that platform in just his long sleeved Mecca shirt, freezing his fine ass off. That's when I knew I was in love."

Ro tried to picture Rugged being sweet and wondered if he would have done the same for Jada. He smiled because he knew that he would have.

"Why you wanna know Ro?"

"Cause…I'm sayin there was this cheerleader at the game tonight."

"Yea?" she asked anxiously.

"Well her name is Jada and I drove her home…and we kicked it, you know, talked and thangs. And I don't know Nae but i'm feelin her. Feelin her like whoa."

"For real?" Nae Nae asked while reaching for the rest of the banana Ro didn't eat.

"Yea, like she's someone who I wouldn't mind being with. I'm talking you know…marriage."

Ro couldn't believe he said that out loud, but hearing it come out of his mouth made it seem even more real.

"Dang, for real Ro? Man you too young to be getting married though."

"Who is getting married?" Rugged asked while walking back into the kitchen and heading straight for the refrigerator.

"Ro in love," Nae Nae said with a smile.

"No, not Romeo," Rugged joked.

Which one was she? Cause I know most of em on the squad."

Romelo didn't answer Nae Nae at first.

"Please don't let it be that little black bitch Rochelle. I can't stand her little dirty ass."

"Naw, you don't know her. She not on Truman's squad. She cheers for Lincoln."

"Lincoln?" Rugged asked.

"Yea," Ro answered, beginning to feel uneasy.

"So does that mean she live in Vector? Tell me she don't live in Vector dog?"

Romelo didn't say anything; he just looked down at his orange and twirled it on the kitchen table.

"Ro…you know…" Rugged began.

"Hold up Rugged, if Ro got feelings for her, then it don't matter where she from," Nae Nae said.

"Oh really! Ok, so would you talk to a nigga from Vector Nae?" he asked her.

"No I wouldn't."

Romelo looked at his sister.

"But that's me...I can't speak for no one else."

"Why cant I? Is there a law somewhere that says that because I live in Foster, I can't love or even like someone from Vector?"

"Yea, there's a law! And it's written in blood. Blood from all them niggas who done died over this shit Ro! Come on now you know. I can't even tell you how many times I have been to a hospital to check a mutha fucka. Or how many funerals yo. You got to do betta then that man."

Romelo sucked his teeth and got up from his chair.

"She the one Rugged, I feel it, I feel it right here," he said while placing his right hand over his heart.

"Just like you feel it for Nae, think what you want tho. I don't give a fuck bout no Vector houses either."

They all remained silent for a few minutes, then Romelo blurted out, "she Terrance sister."

"Huh?" Nae Nae asked.

"Terrance...Big Tee? That's his younger sister."

"Tee? The one Mark killed a whiles back? Cancer's boy? One of the main niggas?" Rugged asked stunned.

"Yea," Ro mumbled.

"Aw shit Ro," Nae Nae said.

"Oh fuck no!" Rugged added.

"I know but, Rugged all that shit, well most of it happened a long time ago..."

79

All three of them were so caught up in the conversation that no one noticed Nature come in. He had been standing there listening to his younger brother talk. Romelo had his back to Nature. Nature walked up to him and shoved him from behind. Romelo flew into Rugged.

"What da fuck?" He asked while turning around.

"It's still happening today Ro!"

"What? What is?" Ro asked puzzled.

"Yall didn't tell him?" Nature asked while looking at Rugged and Nae Nae.

"We were waiting on you."

"Tell me what?"

Nature walked up to Romelo and stuck his finger in his face.

"Didn't I tell you to drive them home? Huh?"

He shoved Romelo again, this time causing him to crash into the kitchen sink.

"Don't put that shit on him Nature!" Nae Nae said.

"Put what on me? What happened?"

"And you standing here talking bout some bitch from Vector?"

"She ain't no bitch Nature," Ro said.

"Look at chu. You know where i'm coming from? I had to drive Mrs. Puente to the city morgue son!"

"A.J.'s mom? Why?"

"Cause Calvin, Rayson and them niggas chased A.J., Butta, and Tre home tonight. They ain't catch Butta or Tre but…"

Romelo sat back down in the Kitchen chair, he looked up at Nature, then at Rugged and finally at Nae Nae.

"The cops told Mrs. Puente that it was an apparent robbery because A.J. didn't have on any sneakers or a jacket. He was slashed across the face they say with either a box cutter or a straight edged razor. They said the quote unfuckin quote robbers left him for dead or some shit and A.J. got up, in some sort of a daze or in shock and he stumbled out into traffic. He was hit by a car and shit. Dead at the fuckin scene. They had to give Mrs. Puente a fuckin sedative, she was a wreck."

Romelo put his head in his hands. He couldn't believe what he was hearing.

"I told you to drive them home!" Nature said while smacking Ro at the back of his head.

"Leave him!" Nae Nae yelled.

"They didn't want to go," Ro said in a soft whisper.

"You always stick with your crew!" Nature yelled.

"Especially when in enemy territory!"

"They didn't want to go!" Ro yelled at Nature.

"Don't you think he hurting? Stop fuckin yelling at him!"

"I'm just sayin Nae, it could a been him...it could have been him."

Romelo got up from the kitchen table and walked towards the front door.

"Romelo where you going?" Nae Nae called out.

He didn't answer, just unlocked the door and let it slam behind him.

"He probably going to the roof and write some fucking poetry."

Nae Nae looked at Nature and sucked her teeth.

"Damn, not little A.J. he was one of dem quiet niggas," Rugged said.

81

"So no arrest right?" Nae Nae asked.

Nature and Rugged both looked at her like she was crazy.

"Of course not. No one's talking, niggs round here are gonna handle it they way, they always do."

"I can't stand this place. I'm not raising my baby up here. Once I have him and graduate, me and Rugged moving from Foster. Right Rugged?"

Rugged just looked at her, he then went to the refrigerator and pulled out two Heinekens. Nae Nae watched him as he opened both bottles and handed one to Nature.

"Ok, whatever...you can stay here. I don't know why niggas think moving up in life or moving away from the P.J's is a bad thing."

"Its all about crew love." Nature said.

"Bump crew love!"

Nae Nae struggled to get up from the table.

"It's all about surviving. I'm gonna go look for Ro."

She waddled to the front door and left apartment 5E.

"Man, what she be doin? Watching Oprah all damn day?" Nature joked.

They both laughed.

"That's my baby tho...so what we gon do? Chill and let the lil niggas handle it? Cause its they beef."

"It's all our beef Rugged."

"True dat."

"Let's go hit dis blunt man."

Nae Nae knew exactly where Romelo was. She pressed floor number 26 in the elevator. Once there she opened the stair case door and climbed the flight and a half of steps that led to the roof. Despite the warning sign on the door, the lock never remained in tact for too long. She smiled at the memory of her and Rugged when they used to sneak up here to "just chill". That's when they called themselves trying to hide their relationship. Nae Nae pushed open the door and spotted Romelo right away. He was sitting on the edge looking towards the river. He turned when he heard her approaching.

"What chu doin up here?" he asked.

She rubbed her stomach and asked him to move over.

"Damn...I forgot how steep those...steps are," she said while breathing heavily.

"What you and Rugged gonna name the baby?"

"I don't know yet, but I was thinking maybe Romelo."

"For real Tanaesha?"

"For real Romelo," she said while rubbing his head.

They sat in silence for a little while. Nae Nae finally broke the silence," you haven't written anything in a while Ro."

"Yea I have."

"Oohhh so you've been holding out on me then. Remember when you used to hide them from Nature. And when he found your poetry book you said they were rap songs and that you were starting a rap group."

They both laughed.

"Yea he had jokes on me for day's man, calling me a punk."

Romelo's grin turned into a grimace.

"I shot her Nae," he blurted out while looking at his sister.

"That was her?" she asked astonished.

"Yea, mannnnnn what am I gonna do?"

"Dang, I remember when you begged me to read that article they had in the newspaper about it. Nature showed it to me and I read it to you."

"I still have that."

"You do?"

"Yea, I don't know why I saved it. And man, who would have thought all these years later I would be..."

"For real. That's creepy and shit. Hey you still got that gun Nature gave you?"

"Naw, I stood right here, where we sitting now and threw it. I was aiming for the river but I don't know where it landed."

"You gonna tell her?"

Ro got up and looked over the edge of the building. He squinted his eyes and tried to make out who was walking in back of A building but he couldn't. He looked down at his feet and saw the letter J he had written on his sneakers earlier.

"I don't know Nae Nae. You think I should?"

"That's a hard one to call Ro. What if she wants to put you in jail for something you did eight years ago?"

"I don't think she would Nae."

Romelo breathed out loud. He found a small broken piece of wood lying on the ground by his foot. He picked it up and threw it as far as he could. He then looked over in the direction of G building.

"Damn, my dawg...A.J."

Nae Nae looked at her younger brother and felt so sorry for him.

"Nature was right yo. I'm sweatin some girl…should have driven all them."

"No, Nature was wrong. That's not your fault Ro."

"A.J. ain't neva really was down for all this madness. All that boy wanted to do was draw super heroes and play ball…" Ro trailed off.

"You never really have been down with it either Romelo. All these people here, all these boys wanna do is go shoot up someone else's projects. Not even realizing they might bump into one of these niggas again someday. Memba that kid from Vector named Mino? He got sent to the island and what? Bumped into Nature and them when Nature was on lock down. They almost killed Mino up there."

"I've been there Nae, I went on the drive bys and graffiti upped houses and all that bullshit. I'm tired of it."

"Me too Ro," she said.

Tanaesha got up and walked towards Romelo.

"But they shouldn't get away with what they did to A.J. He never did shit to no one."

Nae Nae put her arm around her younger brother. They both looked over at G building. Romelo, as hard as he tried not too, began to cry. Tanaesha held him tighter and fought back her own tears.

"I don't know what to tell you Ro. It is fucked up what they did to A.J. Just don't let Nature or anybody pressure you into doin something you don't want. And as far as Jada goes…that's a tough call also" Tanaesha sighed heavily.

"If yall feel about each other the way you say yall do, then maybe Ro, just maybe she will understand and forgive you."

She let go of him and headed towards the roof exit. Once she got back to the staircase door she turned to look at him. Romelo had sat back down and had his head buried in hands. By the way his shoulders were jerking up and down; Taneasha could tell he was crying. Those tears Nae Nae had been holding back finally emerged.

*****

JADA

Jada woke up the next morning with a huge smile on her face. She headed towards the bathroom, but peeked in on her mother first, like she did every morning. Seeing that her mother was still asleep, she went and took a shower and unwrapped her hair. Afterwards, she pulled on her Calvin Klein blue jeans and a pair of ankle high leather black boots. It took Jay a few seconds to decide on what shirt to wear, finally she decided on a long sleeve baby blue, baby phat tee shirt. Jada went down stairs, grabbed the lunch money her mother had left for her off the kitchen table and headed out the front door. She dug in her bag for her house keys and once she found them she turned to lock the front door. When Jada turned back around Cancer was standing directly in front of her. Jada gasped.

"Oh my God Cancer! You scared the mess out of me!"

"Did I?"

"Yea you did. Dang!" she said while placing her right hand over her heart.

"What's up? What you doin here so early?"

She noticed he wasn't moving out of her way, so Jada stepped to the side and walked around him.

"Want me to take you to school?" he asked.

"Oh, naw that's okay, I'm gonna catch up wit Monie and were gonna walk this morning, its too nice out here," she said while looking up at the blue sky.

She began to head towards the front gate. She wondered where Cancer had come from because she knew she didn't hear the squeak of the front gate when she was locking her front door.

"Why you didn't wait for me last night?"

Jada looked at Cancer and noticed the screwface he was giving her.

"Oh, it was kinda getting late and I was getting a little nervous…"

"I told you I would probably be running a little late. You couldn't wait? You get in a car with dat little skinny nigga from Foster!"

Jada was in shock. She couldn't believe he was yelling at her, Cancer had never yelled at her before, never showed her any kind of anger. She felt hurt that he was doing it now.

"Cancer why are you yelling at me?" she asked him, sounding hurt.

"I'm saying Jay, I came and you wasn't there and I know they was playing Foster…I mean playing Truman high last night. I got a little worried when I didn't see you."

He wanted to add that she wasn't representing her hood, was disrespecting it as a matter of fact. She was dissin the memory of her brother Terry and most importantly dissin him. But the hurt look on her face made him bite his tongue instead.

"I'm okay see? And not everybody from Foster is out to kill. But I am sorry for not waiting. I promised I would and that won't happen again."

"You just don't get it babygurl," Cancer said while looking up and down the block.

"Huh? Get what?"

"Nuthin," he said while trying to mask his anger.

"Alright, well I'm out, see you lata Cancer."

Jada opened the front gate and walked down Thornwood Avenue. When she got to the corner she turned to see if Cancer had left or if he was still standing there; He was.

When he noticed that she had turned around he got in his car and drove off.

"Maybe Monica is right...why da hell is he trippin?" she thought.

When she got to Monica's house, Monie was already standing outside waiting on her. Monica had also put on her Calvin Klein blue jeans and ankle black leather boots. Monica chose a black GAP tee shirt to finish off her outfit and pulled her braids back into a ponytail.

"What's up gurl?" Monica asked.

Jada just looked at her friend and smiled.

"Dang, why you cheesin this early in da morning? Is it school or could it be Romeo?"

Jada just laughed.

"I'm gonna meet him today after school. He said to meet him at the bridge."

"Cool, listen girl; can we please go over your guest list again"?

"Why Monie? My party is in a couple of days; the invites have already gone out. Oh my God!"

"What? What happened?"

"I didn't invite Ro."

"Ro? Oh it's Ro now. Well you did just meet him last night Jay."

"I know but...I want him to come. Oh Monie let me tell you. Cancer is trippin man. He was outside the

89

house this morning, breakin on me because I didn't wait for him last night…"

"Monica! Jay!" someone yelled from behind.

They both turned around to see who was calling their names. Nicki came running up to them out of breath.

"Hey Nicki," they said in unison.

"What's up yall? Oh Jay, I'm feelin those boots."

"Thanks."

"Yall hear what happened last night?" Nicki asked.

"No," Monica said.

"What happened?" Jay asked.

"My brother…" Nicki began all to pleased with herself for being the first to spread the news.

"…Was on the phone last night talking to someone, who I don't know. Anyways he said the game last night sucked and…wait didn't you cheer last night Jay?"

"Yea, why?"

"Well he said after Lincoln got they butts beat, he didn't us the word butt tho. After they lost, some of the players from Truman started some shit near Baychester and one of the players ran and got hit by a car."

"What?" Monica asked.

"Yep, right at the foot of the bridge, they say it's all roped off and they still have the white chalk out lined on the street."

Jada automatically thought about Romelo. She hoped he was all right.

"Dang Jay and we was there last night. I wonder which player it was."

Monica and Jay tried to figure out which player it could have been. They grilled Nicki for more info but that's all she said she knew.

"You don't think it was Romeo do you?" Monica asked, full of concern.

"No...I don't think so, he was driving."

"Who's Romeo?" Nicki asked.

Neither of the two bothered to answer her.

"But if he played for Truman, i'm sure he was a friend of Ro's" Jada said.

Jada wanted to go to Romelo now, bump school, she thought. But she didn't know where to find him. She thought about cutting school and just waiting in front of Truman till she saw him. But then she had a frightening thought, what if someone recognized her as being from Vector and they wanted to get some sort of revenge. She didn't know what to do. Monica and Nicki talked about what happened for a little while longer, eventually the subject went from the death of a high school boy to just boys. Jada walked the rest of the way to school in silence, her mind crowded with thoughts about last night and hoping Romelo was okay.

By the time lunch period rolled around, the story had changed dramatically. One version had "the kid from Truman," committing suicide by jumping off the bridge. Another version had to do with an argument over some girls because they had been seen trying to kick it to Octavia on Baychester Ave. And yet another version involved Calvin and Rayson. Jada didn't know what to believe. But she knew she couldn't wait for this day to be over, so she could see him, talk to him and if he needed or wanted, hold him.

Monica sat down next to Jay at lunch; she looked at her friend, and then patted her on the back.

"Huh?"

"Nothing, you just so quiet Jay. What's up?"

"It's everything Monie, with Cancer flippin on me this morning, then hearing about that boy getting hit by a car, and I keep thinking about Terry…"

"Yea, I heard it was A.J."

"A.J.?" Jay asked.

"Yea, the point guard. Remember I asked you to put him on the invite list?"

"Damn." Jay hung her head low, causing some of her hair to fall into her eyes.

"Popo was here earlier too, they were questioning mostly the basketball team," Monica said while spooning applesauce into her mouth.

"I hope there isn't another Vector/Foster war Monica. I can't really take another one of those," Jay said while brushing the hair out of her eyes.

"I know boo boo. These niggas round here make me sick."

Monica looked around the cafeteria and spotted Rayson.

"I haven't seen Calvin today but there's Rayson. Jay?"

"Yea?"

"Do you think you should invite Romeo? I mean with errything that's going on."

"I thought about that too Monie. I don't know…maybe not."

"Well just don't invite Calvin and his little crew."

"I didn't and I'm hoping Cancer don't come now either."

Two fifteen finally arrived, Jada practically ran out of Lincoln's front door. She headed towards the bridge, walking as fast as possible. She remembered Ro said to meet him at the foot of the bridge but she neglected to ask which side. The side that led to Foster or the side that led to Vector? She figured it would be the Foster side so Jada climbed the bridge steps. Once at the top, Jada took notice of how raggedy the bridge looked. The wire link fence was rusted and trash was littered everywhere. There were patches of grass in some spots and large bushes in others. She wished the city would tear it down, or at least build a better one. Jada thought about all of the violence that occurs on the bridge. Fights after school, robberies, and who knows what else. She wondered why the bridge was allowed to exist this long and no one ever did anything about it. She stopped for a second to look at the huge Mack trucks that drove on the freeway beneath. This is the only thing Vector has in common with Foster, she thought. Jada began to look around for Romelo but she didn't see him.

"What's up Jay?" someone yelled out.

Jada smiled and waved. She crossed over the bridge and began to descend the steps. A lot of kids were standing around, Jada noticed as she approached the bottom of the steps. She slowed down, and hoped there wasn't any blood on the ground or that white chalk outline. As she got closer she noticed most of the bottom platform was roped off with yellow police tape.

Someone had broken the tape, now it just flapped in the light September wind. Some kids stopped and looked, some pointed, one even bent down, and while eyeing a spot on the ground, yelled out," I think this is blood here!" Jada glanced but kept on walking. She still didn't see Ro; she leaned against a light post and decided to make that her spot for now.

She made small talk with a few people she recognized that were on their way home. She also noticed a police cruiser drive past her more then once. Off in the distance, across the four-lane street and past Truman, she could see Foster. The buildings stood much taller then those in Vector. She wondered which building Romelo lived in. The thought of him made her smile.

"Romelo Jones," she said out loud. Jada then looked at her watch; it read 3:10pm. She hadn't realized that she had been waiting for him for almost an hour. Most of the school kids were gone now, just a few hung around talking and smoking Newport's. Jada began to get really nervous; she felt that something was wrong. She realized that she really didn't know Romelo that well. But she also felt she knew him well enough to know he wouldn't leave her here, standing, waiting on him. She felt like kicking herself for not getting his phone number or address.

"Something must be wrong," she said out loud.

Jada decided to head back up the steps and towards home. She looked around once more, and with no luck began to climb the steps. While looking up, she spotted Nicki coming down.

"I thought that was you. What's up gurl? What chu doin?" Nicki asked.

"What's up Nicki? I was waitin for someone but…" Jada trailed off. "Anyway what you doin ova here?"

"I was headed to Truman," Nicki replied.

"Truman? What for?"

"My dad works there. He does custodial work."

"Say word…I didn't know that."

"It's nothing to brag about Jay. I paged him, I'm a hit him up for some money so I could get them new Nikes."

"Oh."

"Want to walk with me? It'll take me like five minutes. Then we could walk back to Vector together."

Jada was more then pleased to go with Nicki. Maybe, just maybe, she thought, she would bump into Romelo. They crossed the street and headed towards Truman high school.

"Let's go round back. That's gonna be the only door open, the one leading to the gym in the basement. That's where my pops office is."

Jada looked up at the high school, then around the area. She realized she had never been over here. Never been anywhere near Foster. And she only lived ten maybe 15 minutes away. Doesn't look any different from Vector, just bigger buildings, she thought.

On their way into the back entrance of Truman, Nicki and Jay bumped into a small group of students coming out. The girls in the group eyed both Jada and Nicki suspiously. One, after having looked Jay up and down, grabbed her obvious boyfriend and pushed him. Jada wasn't interested in any beef so she avoided eye contact. Nicki, on the other hand, laughed out loud and said," bitches is funny." Jada however did notice that two of the guys had on Truman Basketball jerseys. Could there have been a game today or maybe practice, that would explain his no show, she thought. They walked down the corridor, past the gym, towards the custodial office.

"I'll be right back Jay," Nicki said while knocking on the door then letting herself in. Jada could hear voices coming from the gym. She walked back down the corridor and into the huge gymnasium. She immediately recognized the basketball coach from last night. He was sitting in the stands with a couple of players around him. One guy looked as if he was crying; he had pulled his jersey up to cover his eyes. Another player just kept patting him on the back. Jada looked around hoping she would see Romelo. When she didn't, she turned and headed for the exit. She bumped into Tre.

"Pardon me," Tre said.

"I'm sorry," she said.

She looked Tre in the face and recognized him from the night before. As Tre passed her she placed her hand on his arm to get his attention.

"Excuse me, can I ask you something?"

"Yea?"

"I'm looking for Romelo, you seen him?"

"Ro? Who you?"

"I'm Jada…a friend of his," Jada replied.

"Yea? Well I was just about to go check him, afta I tell coach something. You can roll wit me, to his crib."

"Oh, okay," Jay, said.

Jay and Tre walked past Truman, through Foster houses. They made small talk along the way until they came to A building. Tre knocked on the door to

Apt.5E. Tanaesha answered the door and greeted Tre with a hug. They remained in that embrace for more then a few seconds. She rubbed Tre's back and whispered something to him. She then let him go but looked him in the eyes.

"You all right?" she asked him.

"Yea...im cool," he said while wiping a tear out of the corner of his eye.

It wasn't until then that Nae Nae noticed Jada standing there.

"How you doin?" she asked Jada.

"I'm fine."

"Jay this is Ro's sister. Nae, this is Jay, she looking for Ro. Where he at? He ain't come to school today."

"Yea, I know...he taking it all kinda bad. Jay? Is that short for Jada?" Nae asked while looking at Jada.

"Yea it is."

Nae Nae smiled at her, "oh I heard about you."

"You did?" Jada asked surprised.

"No doubt, it's all good too. Tre, Ro is up on the roof. He has been there all night. I'm glad it's not cold out yet cause he would have froze by now."

"Aiiight, well i'm a come by lata then. Tell him I rolled thru."

Jada thought to herself, there's no way she could leave without at least laying her eyes on him. His sister said he was taking it hard, she had to go to him.

"Do you mind if I wait for him Nae Nae?" Jada asked.

"No I don't mind. As a matter of fact, why don't you just go upstairs. I think that would be cool. He expecting me to bring him something to eat but I'm not his damn servant, tell him that and give this to him."

Nae Nae gave Jada a red apple to give to Romelo. After thanking Tre and getting directions from Nae Nae on how to get to the roof, Jada made her way up. She read the warning sign on the roof door then pushed it open. The sun hit her in the eyes blinding her for a few seconds. She raised her right hand to give shade.

Once she found a shaded spot she stepped into it. Then she saw him; Romelo was standing against the railing with his back to her. Jada looked Romelo up and down from head to toe. She noticed he still had on the green polo hoodie, but had changed into a matching green pair of Polo sweat pants. He had his white Jordan's on and a white stocking cap on his head. Beside him, lying near his foot was his basketball and two notebooks. The sight of Romelo Jones made Jada feel weak in the knees. She knew she wanted to be with him, some where down the line, marry him and eventually start a family. She watched him pull his sweat pants up but they fell right back into their original sagging position. She didn't know why she was so nervous right now. What if he didn't want to see her? What if he didn't want to deal with her solely on the basis of where she lived? Only one way to find out she thought. Jada took a step closer to Ro and cleared her throat.

"Nae come here…tell me if you can tell who this is, just by the way he walk," he said with his back still to Jada.

"Nae Nae said to give you this," Jada said while holding the apple out to him.

Romelo turned around with the quickness. He stepped down off the small railing and just looked at her.

"Close you mouth Romelo Jones," She said with a smile.

She began walking towards him but he was up on her before she could take her second step. He held her in a strong embrace; Jada could feel Romelo's body begin to shake. He dug his head deeper into her shoulder and she held him tighter. The thought of Romelo crying on her shoulder bought tears to Jada's eyes. Ro was saying something to her but she couldn't make it out. She felt his body get limp and suddenly he dropped to his knees.

"Jada…I need to tell you something," he said softly while looking down at the ground.

Jada dropped to her knees in front of him and lifted his face with both her hands.

"It's okay," she whispered. "I heard about your friend, i'm sorry Ro."

He saw that tears had escaped the corners of her eyes and rolled down her cheeks.

"Why are you crying?"

"Cause your crying."

"Jay…I love you," Romelo said.

She wiped his tears with her fingers and smiled.

"I love you too Romelo."

They kissed, but unlike the night before, this kiss seemed more passionate. Ro put his tongue in her mouth and Jay responded by doing the same. They separated and for a few seconds and just looked into each other's eyes.

"I wanna marry you," he said.

"You do?"

"Yea…I do."

They kissed again, Ro reached around and pulled her closer to him. He let his hands slide down her back until they rested on her butt. Jada stopped kissing him and looked him in the eyes. Ro stood up quickly, thinking he did something wrong. Jada stood up as well and took her leather jacket out from inside her bookbag and laid it down on the roof pavement. Romelo caught on to what she was doing, and quickly pulled off his sweat hood and laid it down as well. He walked to the exit door and picked up a large piece of plywood that was leaning up against the wall. He wedged it under the doorknob and kicked it a couple of times until it stayed in place. Once he was assured no one would be able to push open the staircase door, he turned to face her. She had already removed her shirt and had it folded neatly, sitting on her bookbag with the apple. She stood there in a black bra. Ro glanced at her shoulder, searching for any remnants of that night eight years ago but saw none. He took his jersey off, folded it and placed it where a pillow might go. Jada looked at his chest and felt weak again. His six-pack made her yearn for him. She lay down on the makeshift bed and Ro lay on top of her. They made love that sunny September afternoon, and as the sun shined down on them, nothing else seemed to matter. Not Cancer, not Nature, and certainly not Foster and not Vector. Afterwards, they both sat with their backs against the wall, sharing the apple. Jada kept smiling as she listened to him describe his grandmother to her.

"So we take care of her, she has heart problems but she will love you and you already met Nae Nae, oh man you gotta meet Rugged. He the father of Nae

Nae's baby. He mad cool, bought me them new Jordan's," he said while pointing to his sneakers.

"Oh, the one's with the letter J on em?" she asked.

"Yea," he said with a laugh.

"I noticed that last night but I didn't want to ask. You might have said they stood for Jennifer or Janel or Jamquita."

"Jamquita?" he asked. And they both laughed out loud.

Romelo's face suddenly grew solemn as he looked up at the sky.

"Yea...and I want to introduce you to my big brother Nature. I have been avoiding him, he blames me for A.J.'s death and I blame myself also."

"No, don't do that! Don't blame yourself Ro; it was not your fault. Your brother is wrong," she said while grabbing his hand.

"I should have driven them all home last night Jay."

"Ro, you didn't push A.J. in front of that car. You did what you were supposed to do because this is meant." She pointed to herself and then to him.

"Isn't that what you told me last night? We're meant? Destined?"

Romelo smiled at her then leaned over and kissed her soft lips.

"Your right Jada...cause I almost killed you and you didn't die. God kept you here for me...for us." Romelo started rambling and stuttering so much so that Jada couldn't understand what he was talking about.

"Huh? You almost killed me? What are you talking about?" she asked, her voice filled with confusion.

Romelo stood up and pulled his jersey over his head. He avoided eye contact with her but began to explain that night, eight years ago when their paths first crossed. He told her that at nine he really didn't understand the beef between Vector and Foster, but he knew he wasn't supposed to like or associate with anyone from over there. He explained how he doesn't really remember shooting the door, actually pulling the trigger but he remembers the noise, how loud it was.

"Swiss cheese, that's what I remember. I remember your door looking like Swiss cheese with all them holes in it. I didn't want to be there but Nature said I had to and said we wasn't gonna hurt nobody...I didn't know...I...I...didn't realize until last night when I drove you home..." He looked over at Jada and she was looking up at him with a look of utter shock on her face.

"Oh my God," she said while placing her hands over her mouth.

"I saw you. I looked out my window, got down on my knees and watched you. I remember thinking how you looked my age and I thought you was holding that gun funny, like the wrong way or something..."

She trailed off and sat silent for a few seconds. Jada looked down at her feet and continued, "I mean I know Terry used to get in trouble a lot. Cops was always knocking on our door either bringing him home or asking about him, I used to hear him and Cancer and them talk bout jumping this person or robbing that person. When I was in the hospital they thought I was sleeping but I wasn't. I listened to Terry yell about how Foster was going to pay...He may not have been right but he didn't deserve to die that way." Jada lowered her head and closed her eyes. Romelo walked over to the books he had laying on the ground and picked up one. He began searching for something he had written earlier. When he found it he walked back over to Jada and began reading.

My whole life has been turned upside down
I never knew the meaning of want,
Till I found
My destiny, my complete
My rose growing in the middle of concrete
I want to uproot her and plant her solidly in my ground
Water her…nurture her
Show her true love that's solid, true love that's sound
Love her like no other can
Right here, right now I take a stand
I pledge to forever be her man…
My girl, my calmness in the middle of a storm
My world, my reason to wake in the morn
My boo, my savior
My rose, My Jada

When he finished he got down on his knees in front of her and grabbed her right hand. She lifted her head and looked at him with tears in her eyes.

"Jay…I'm so sorry. Please, please forgive me. I know we just met and I know you have no reason to but forgive me. I feel like I have known you my whole life and…" he trailed off.

"And what Ro?" she asked while squeezing his hand tight.

"And I want to marry you…will you? Will you marry me Jada?"

Without any hesitation, Jada replied, "Yes Romelo, I will."

Romelo stood up straight and with a look of pure astonishment he looked down at her.

"Are you serious?"

"Why wouldn't I be?" she said while standing up.

"You don't hate me?"

"No I don't hate you...I love you."

Ro grabbed her and spun her around. Jada squealed.

He suddenly stopped and put her back on her feet. Ro then pulled the gold ring with the letter R encrusted in diamonds on the top that he wore on his index finger off. He got down on one knee and took Jay's hand.

"This is the only ring I got right now. But until I can get you the right one, you can wear this. It means a lot to me, Nature got it for me."

Jada just stood there and cheesed. She held up her hand after he slipped it on her finger and looked at it. When she lowered her hand the ring fell off. They both laughed.

"I can hang it on my chain okay?"

"Aiight, damn I don't believe this. Man this is like whoa! I know of course not right away. We got school, graduate next year..."

"Why not right away," she interrupted.

"I mean I know it would take some planning and things like that but...I just want to be with you Ro. Everyday, all day."

Jada walked over to the basketball that was lying on the pavement and picked it up. She began dribbling the ball.

"So what you got to say to that Mr. Jones?"

"You ain't got no game Mrs. Jones."

He bumped her from behind.

"Ohhhhh you play dirty I see."

Jada dribbled the ball off her foot and lost it, Ro grabbed it and began dribbling.

"And I say to that, why not right away."

He bounced the ball between his legs and bought it back to his right side.

Jada tried to take the ball from him but was unsuccessful. She poked him in the ribs and then grabbed the ball.

"Punk," she said with a grin.

"Ohh i'm a punk?" Ro laughed out loud. "I think they would call that a foul."

Jay dropped the ball and walked over to Ro.

"I think they would call this a kiss."

She put her lips on his while holding him tight.

Jada unbuttoned her jeans for the second time that afternoon. And as the world went on about its business, Romelo and Jada made love, both knowing that what they were feeling, felt too good to be considered wrong. Afterwards, while pulling her shirt over her head, Jada gasped.

"Oh my God!"

"What?"

"I forgot, my birthday is Saturday and I'm supposed to meet Monie so we can go get our dresses for the party."

"Say word, your birthday?"

"Ro you got to come okay? Say you'll be there," she pleaded.

"I want to…do you think I should with…you know. I mean i'm not tryna cause no trouble on your day."

"I know." Jay grabbed her jacket and knapsack. "I betta go, my mother is gonna kill me. I'm gonna hafta lie, say I had to attend an unannounced practice or something like that."

"Kay, listen, I'm gonna come, but i'm not going to stay long. I'm not tryna see none of them niggas yo. Just long enough to wish you a happy birthday. I don't want no beef boo."

"Good," she said with a smile.

"And long enough for a kiss too?"

"Oh no doubt," he answered.

"You don't even hafta come in the center. I'll have Monie look out for you and when you arrive she can come get me. Maybe I can convince you to give me at least one dance."

"A dance and a kiss? You pushin it kid."

Jada playfully hit him on the head.

"Come on; let me see if I can get someone to give you a ride home. And then I have to find Nature, me and him need to talk." Ro turned and looked at Jada, "when you wanna do this," he asked her.

"Ummmm…how bout after my birthday," she said nervously.

"When?"

"I don't know, that Sunday or Monday after school."

"You sure?" Ro asked.

"I'm sure," Jay replied.

They both smiled at each other.

"Ok so we got a lot we hafta do then. I'm a talk to Rugged and Nae; they might be able to tell us where we need to go. Maybe even ask coach."

Ro picked up his hoodie and put it on, he then grabbed his ball and they headed towards the exit.

"Oh wait," he said while running towards the books he left lying on the ground. He walked towards the doors, bent down and removed a small link grating from the wall. He pulled out a dusty covered bookbag and unzipped it. Ro placed the two books in the bag, zippered it back up and put it neatly back in its hiding place.

"You come up here a lot?" she asked when he was finished.

"Yea...I come to the rooftop to write or think or too just get away. But mostly I come for that."

Ro pointed to the sunset. Him and Jada walked hand in hand to the railing and looked up at the sky.

"See, look at that. It's like velvet. Velvet skies."

The sun seemed to be surrounded by a burgundy blanket of clouds. The once bright and vibrant sky now appeared to be serene as the sun prepared to say goodbye at least for now.

"It's cool up here. Can this be our place?" Jay asked.

"Yea. I consider myself away from Foster when I come up here. Away but not to far away. You know what I mean? I never really wanted to leave altogether, not until now. Come on let me introduce you to my grandmother then get you home."

Jada smoothed down her hair with her hands.

"Do I look ok?"

"Mannnn, you are fine!"

107

Jada smiled as they headed down the stairs and to apt. 5E.

*****

JADA

When Jada arrived home, her mother was waiting for her in the kitchen. She heard Jay's keys in the front door and called out to her.

"Jay?"

"Yea mommy?"

"Come here please."

Jada walked into the kitchen and saw that her mother was baking and had the television on loudly in the living room. Jada paused to see which movie it was. "Apple pie and an old black classic, i'm in trouble," Jada thought.

"What you baking mommy?" she asked innocently.

"Apple pie."

"Dang mommy you haven't baked an apple pie in a good while. You need some help?"

"No, I'm almost finished...why are you just now getting home from school?"

Jada looked up at the kitchen clock; it read 6:47p.m.

"I'm sorry mommy, we had an unannounced practice after school today and it lasted long cause Sondra couldn't get the routine down and..."

"Umm hmmm," her mother interrupted.

Jada continued, "Then I had paged Cancer to see if he could come get me and I had to wait on him."

Mary put the knife she had in her hand down on the kitchen counter and looked over at her daughter.

"What?" Jay asked nervously.

"Since when are you in the business of lying to me?"

"Huh?"

"Cancer called here five times, looking for you. What's going on Jay?"

Jada was confused.

"He did?" she asked.

"Yes he did. So you obviously were not with him. Again, I ask, why are you coming home so late?"

"Ok mommy, I'm sorry I just lied. I met this guy the other night at the game, his name is Romelo and we just hung out after school, I'm sorry," she said while lowering her eyes.

"Romelo? What kind of name is that?"

Jada just smiled.

"So do you normally hang out after school with a boy and not call me?"

"No."

"Jay you know better then that. You are not allowed to hang out after school. You come right home, no excuses, you know this."

"I know mommy...I'm sorry. Mommy what Cancer want?"

"I don't know, he asked where you were and kept saying he would try again later. That boy made me nervous. Plus Monica's mother told me some boy got hit by a car the other night after having been in a fight." Mary shook her head side to side. "I'm praying for his family".

"Yea...oh man! I hafta call Monie, I was..."

"You were supposed to go pickup your dress today. You're going to have to do that tomorrow."

"Yea. Ok i'm going to go start my homework and then call her," Jay said while heading towards the kitchen doorway.

"Wait a minute Jay. Come here."

Jada turned to look at her mother then walked towards her. Mary held her arms out.

"Gimmie hug," she said.

Jay gladly walked into her mothers open arms and held her tight. She wanted to tell her all about Romelo but she felt like now was not the right time. Maybe tomorrow, she thought. They walked into the living room together, arms still around each other.

"Your father called today."

"He did?"

"Yea. I told him you weren't here but to call you back tonight."

"So is that why you have on Lady Sings the Blues and baking apple pie?"

Mary laughed.

"Did he say if he was coming to my party or not?"

"Nope, we actually didn't get around to that."

"Yall didn't argue did yall?"

"No we didn't argue Jay," Mary answered.

"Good...I didn't mean to make you worried mommy."

"I know baby, go do your homework. Want me to rewind and we can watch this over some apple pie?"

"Yea, that's cool. Just fast forward on the part when piano man dies, you know I hate that part," Jada said.

Mary and Jada began imitating Diana Ross.

"Piano man gone...we go home now?"

They both fell out laughing.

111

"Gone girl, the pie will be ready by the time you get finished," Mary said in between laughs.

Jada ran upstairs to her room and threw herself down on the bed. She looked up at the ceiling and smiled. She smiled so hard her cheeks began to hurt.

"Mrs. Romelo Jones," she said out loud.

She ran her hands up and over her thighs and then over the front of her jeans.

"Oh my God!" she squealed with delight.

Jay jumped up and reached for her phone.

"Wait till I tell Monie."

"Talk to me," is how Monica answered her phone.

"Ok you need to sit down, because I got something to tell you," Jada said excitedly.

"Jay! I'm a hurt you gurl! Weren't we pose to pick up our dresses this afternoon?"

"Yea, but wait…"

Monica sucked her teeth. "Jay Cancer called here like three times, asking me all sorts of questions."

The smile on Jada's face quickly subsided.

"For real?" she asked.

"No, for fake. Of course for real! What is up wit that?"

"I don't know what's up with that. My mother just told me he called here like five times also."

"Dang!"

"I'm starting to believe what you said about Cancer liking me…but I don't get it, he has a girl." Jada said.

"And? Shoot, he said his girl Keisha; she's the one who told him that you were in Foster with Tre, going to Romelo's house. Man Cancer was pissed."

Jada sucked her teeth, and then took a deep breath.

"I don't know Monie, I don't want Cancer coming to the party. He buggin and I don't want any shit."

"Oh oh I know you not cursing?" Monica joked.

Jada laughed. "I'm serious Monie."

"I know boo."

"Romelo's gonna come tho."

"Oh yea, you got to tell me about you hooking up today with Romeo. Is that why you got home late?

Jada spent the next 40 minutes on the phone, telling her best friend everything that happened on the rooftop of A building in Foster houses.

"Oh snap!" was all that Monica could say.

After swearing Monica to secrecy and promising to meet up tomorrow morning, Jada finally hug up the phone. She then realized that it was Friday and that meant no homework so she went to go get her mother and some apple pie. She looked into her mother's bedroom first and found her fast asleep on her bed with the Daily News sprawled out on top of her. Jada kissed her mother on the forehead and turned out the light.

ROMELO

Romelo walked into Rugged and Nae Nae's bedroom and sat on the bed.

"Jada is pretty Ro," Nae said while flipping through the latest issued of XXL magazine.

"She is," he said with a huge smile.

"Ummm hmmmm, and what was yall doing up on the roof, all this time?"

"Talking," Ro replied while looking out the window.

He then walked over to the baby crib that Rugged bought and picked up a stuffed lavender elephant.

"Rugged gonna spoil this baby."

"I know," Nae said with a laugh.

"He's a good man Nae…good to you. That's what I want to be, good to Jay."

"Yea he is, I just wish he would quit hustling, that shit makes me nervous. But he claims he's just starting to blow up and to give him at least two more years. Where gonna start our own business and get the hell out of Foster."

"I hear you, I'm gonna leave Foster too, me and Jay wanna get married."

"Say word!" Nae Nae said while struggling to get to her feet.

"You alright?" Ro asked while giggling at the sight of Nae's belly poking out of her too tight baby phat tee shirt.

"How come you never bought any maternity clothes?"

Because I didn't think I was gonna get this big. I swear this baby gonna be a preemie, he act like he wanna drop now. But don't try to change the subject, did you say get married?"

"Yea, I love her."

"That is good Ro, i'm happy for you little man."

Nae Nae walked over to Ro and gave him a hug.

"Thanks."

"So when? No time soon right?"

"Soon Nae Nae, and please don't tell me i'm too young. I want Rugged to be my best man when we do."

"You are too young but…"

Nae Nae rubbed her stomach and then looked at Ro.

"You know that's gonna make Nature mad right?"

"Yea I know but i'm saying Nae, I feel like Rugged has always been more of a brother then Nature."

"Nat loves you Ro, he just…I guess wants you to be more like him, more like the niggas round here, shit eat and breathe Foster."

"There's more then Foster Nae."

"I know boo boo."

Ro put the elephant back in the crib.

"Where's Nature, you know?"

"Should be by the courts on the wall," she answered.

"Aight." He rubbed Nae Nae's stomach and she swung at him but missed.

"Love ya," he said while running out the room.

"Don't do that, I hate that shit," She rolled her eyes in his direction, and then it dawned on her what Romelo had just said.

"Wait Ro, what do you mean soon? How soon?" she yelled out, but he was already gone.

Romelo walked to the basketball courts. The schoolyard courts remained well lit, despite a couple of busted streetlights. He passed the police sub station and saw no one inside. He remembered when they kept a cop manned there twenty-four seven. A few people sat around on parked cars in front of the courts. A small crowd was gathered at the wall, Ro headed in their direction.

"Sup Ro?" Butta called out.

"What up man," Ro said while giving Butta some dap and a hug.

"What's goin on?" Ro asked while looking around for Nature.

"Ain't nuthin…we was just talking bout A.J. and shit."

The mention of A.J.'s name made Ro's eyes water, he turned his back to Butta, not wanting him to see the tears that began to form. When he looked up the street he saw Nature, Rugged, Tre, Lil Mickey and a few other cats headed in their direction.

"We all going to Mrs. Jimenez crib to pay our respects," Butta said.

Tre walked up to Ro and gave him a hug.

"Sup dawg?"

"Sup Tre."

"What da deal Ro?" Lil Mickey asked while giving Ro some dap.

"Nuthin man," Ro responded.

Every one exchanged pounds; a blunt was lit and passed around. Ro leaned on the car next to Butta. Nature puffed twice on the blunt and then walked over to Romelo and held it up to his face.

"Naw…I don't want none," Ro said.

Nature sucked his teeth then passed it to Butta. He spit on the ground then walked back over to Rugged and the rest.

"Aye yo, Lee called me earlier today. That boy wants me to send him a care package and shit," Nature said to Rugged. "You coming with me to visit him next weekend?"

"You alright Ro?" Butta asked.

"Naw son, not really…I feel bad yo; like it's my fault A.J. is dead."

Butta took a long pull, blew out the smoke slowly and watched it disappear, he then shook out his dreads and looked at his friend.

"Yea, that's what Nature is saying, that it's your fault, if you had driven us home, A.J. would be here today. But naw son, it's not your fault, I don't believe that. I believe shit like this is already written. It was just A.J.'s time to bounce…that's what I think." Butta took another long pull off the blunt.

"Word?" Ro asked. "Is that what you believe?"

"Yea, but of course that doesn't mean its not fucked up dat he gone, that was my nigg and that don't let them niggas off the hook either," Butta said in between exhaling smoke.

Ro picked up his ball and began bouncing it. He thought about what Butta just said.

"Yo remember that time A.J. tried to dunk on me?" He asked.

Butta and Tre started laughing.

"Yea, he tripped or something and fell flat on his face, chipped his tooth and everythang."

Everyone else joined them in laughter except Nature.

"I wrote that down right here on the ball, the date and all," Ro said.

He pointed to his ball and the letters A.J. and a date that was written on it.

"That boy had skills tho. I loved playing pick up with him. I wish he was here now so we could go at it, a lil one on one," Ro said while dribbling the ball between his legs.

He walked up to Butta and took the blunt from him; he held it between his two lips then snatched the ball from Romelo.

"Well he ain't here now is he?" Nature asked while shooting Ro an evil look.

Nature crossed the street with the ball in his hands, when he got to the court he turned around to face Romelo. He pulled on the blunt then threw the remainder to the ground.

"But I am Ro, so what's up?" Nature yelled across the street. He crawled thru the hole in the wire link fence and stepped up onto the court.

"Aww shit," Lil Mickey said.

The small crowd began to cross the street.

"Ignore him Ro," Tre said.

Romelo stared straight at Nature.

"Naw, not this time," he said.

He crossed the street also and climbed on the courts. Nature unzipped his leather Avirex jacket then took it off. He then took off his Nautica shirt and threw both to the ground. Romelo snatched his white Yankee's baseball cap off his head and tossed it to Butta.

"Aight son, lets go," Nature said with a grin.

"To five Ro."

"Whateva yo, just take this ass whipping like the man you claim to be."

Nature bounced the ball hard then threw it to Romelo, hitting him in the chest with it.

"Check pussy."

Ro threw it back and the second Nature caught the ball he drove to the basket. Ro immediately d'ed up. Nature dribbled then released and Ro smacked the ball away.

"Oohhh!" The crowd yelled.

"Aight punk," Nature said.

Romelo retrieved the ball.

"Oh I'm a punk now huh?"

"Well you sho nuff not a fuckin man!"

Romelo dribbled low and stood face to face with his bigger brother.

"What makes me a man Nature? Huh? You tell me since you got it down. Smoking and selling? Carrying a gat? Huh? Shit! I have been doing that since the age of eight, thanks to you!" Romelo yelled.

"Sitting on the roof and writing poetry all damn day sure nuff don't make you one."

A few snickers of laughter could be heard coming from the small crowd. Ro drove to the basket, knocking Nature down in the process. He scored the first basket. He then kicked the ball to Nature.

"You should thank me," Nature said while getting to his feet. He dribbled the ball and backed into Romelo. He tried to fake to his left but Ro read his every move. He reached around and stole the ball. He looked Nature in the eyes and backed up from him.

"Thank you for what Nature? For making me feel bad cause I'm not you? For making me feel bad cause I didn't drive A.J. home?" Ro squared up and let the ball go. He scored again.

"Two!" someone yelled from the crowd.

Nature caught the ball as it came down out of the net.

"No one blamed you for not being there for Saquan. Jada told me…"

Nature looked at Romelo," I don't give a fuck what dat bitch told you!" He then hurled the ball as far as he could. Everyone watched as it flew in the air, disappearing on the rooftop of P.S.160 Elementary School.

"Damn! Woooooo, I should have challenged his ass to some football," Nature joked to the small crowd while standing with his arms spread wide open. He turned his back to Ro and began to walk off the court laughing. Before anyone knew what was happening, Ro had charged at Nature, knocking him to the ground. He tried to put Nature in a headlock but couldn't. Nature wriggled out from under him, grabbed Ro and pushed him down on his back to the ground. Nature jumped up quick, he then put his heavy timberland boot on Ro's neck. Ro struggled to remove Natures foot but couldn't.

"You may be able to beat me at ball, but you can't beat my ass Ro!" Nature yelled down to him. He applied more pressure, Ro stopped trying to free himself and just lay there.

"Aiight chill Nature!" Rugged yelled out.

"And you can thank me for always tryin to protect yo ass...and for loving you." Nature lifted his foot off of Ro's neck and walked away from him.

"We going to Mrs. Jimenez house or what?" he asked no one in particular while putting his jersey back on. The small crowd began to disperse and head towards G building. Rugged walked over to Romelo and helped him off the ground.

"I can't stand him," Ro said while holding his throat.

Just then one of Rugged's customers approached both of them and asked Rugged for four yellow tops. While Rugged made the sell, Romelo searched for his hat. He found it and placed in back on his head. He and Rugged walked towards A.J.'s building.

"I'm serious Rug, I hate him."

"No you don't. You love him and he loves you, trust. That's all he talks about, you and Nae. Protecting yall, making sure gammy is aight. You know he feels that's his job since yall ain't got pops around."

"Well he not my father!" Ro said, still holding his throat.

"True but he the one buys the food to feed yo ass. You know he didn't want to be out here on the corner wit me. He could have kept his bullshit job at that supermarket, but that wasn't enough to feed you and Nae and gammy. Shit and we ain't even got to clothes. Who keep you geared up in all dat designer shit?

Aight?? We waiting for you to enter the NBA just so you could pay us back."

Romelo didn't say anything, but he did think about what Rugged was saying.

"Oh did I mention rent? Bills?"

"Alright Rugged…I hear you."

"Yea, I thought that you might. So yall need to quit the arguing and just have each other's back. Cause if shit happened to you, he'd be lost and vice versa."

They entered the lobby of G building. Everyone else had already gone upstairs. The elevator doors opened up, they both stepped in. Romelo pressed button number 9. Then took a deep breath.

"I hate this shit!" Rugged said.

The doors opened up on floor nine. They stepped out and headed straight for apartment 9A. But before they could reach the door, they heard noise coming from the staircase. Rugged opened the door and looked inside. Nature and a few others were sitting on the steps smoking. A bottle of vodka was being passed around; Nature grabbed it and poured a little out on the staircase ground.

"For those who are not here. Yo they got mad family over. I paid my respects, his lil crew in there now."

"Aight, i'm a be right back. Yall niggas don't act a fool with dat vodka, save me some," Rugged said.

"No doubt."

Romelo rang the doorbell and immediately the door was opened. An older gentleman looked at them sadly, and then stepped to the side to let them past.

"I'm sorry for your lost," Rugged said while shaking his hand. The older gentleman just nodded at him. They passed a few more people in the hallway, then made their way to the kitchen. Mrs. Jimenez was seated at the kitchen table discussing funeral arrangements with relatives. When she looked up she noticed Romelo and Rugged standing in the kitchen doorway. She let out a faint gasp of air and squeezed her eyes shut. Two tears rolled down each cheek. When she opened her eyes again she stood up and had to steady herself by leaning on the kitchen table. Romelo had never seen anything else but a smile on Mrs. Jimenez face. The woman he was looking at now did not appear to be the same person. Her eyes were blood shot and swollen. Her hair had been pulled into a bun, but several strands escaped and were now just hanging down, mingling with the tears that soaked her cheeks. She grabbed Romelo and hugged him tight.

"Aye Romelo," she said.

"I'm so sorry Mrs. Jimenez," he whispered.

She let go of him, then announced, "everyone deese ez Romelo, Angelo's good friend. Angelo loved him some Romelo, he would come home and tell me all about the games."

Romelo nodded at everyone in the kitchen, he then leaned in and kissed Mrs. Jimenez on her cheek.

"I'm so so sorry," he said again.

"I know," she said while squeezing his hand.

She then let go and gave Rugged a hug as well. Rugged felt her body get limp, he helped her back to her chair at the table.

"Ti Ti, you need to get some rest. You haven't slept since yesterday," a young woman who was at the stove dishing some red beans and rice onto a paper plate said. Romelo backed out of the kitchen; he decided to go look for Butta, Lil Mickey and Tre. He found them in A.J.'s bedroom.

"What chall doin?" he asked.

"Nuthin," Butta replied.

"Say word. Look at this," Tre said.

He passed Butta A.J.'s photo album and pointed to a picture.

"Memba when we took that? Some time last year I think."

Butta began to smile, "Hell yea, we was goin to the movies."

Let me see?" Ro asked with his hand held out.

Butta passed him the album. Ro sat down on the bed and looked intently at the photo. In it he stood between Butta and A.J. while Lil Mickey and Tre knelt down in front of them. Butta was cheesing hard enough to show off his gold fronts while Ro, A.J. and Lil Mickey showed off the new kicks they had bought earlier that day. Ro looked at A.J. And smiled.

"Pretty boys," he said.

"Yea that's what they called us, jealous muthafuckas," Lil Mickey said.

"We never even saw the whole movie, somebody started some shit with somebody else, and we all ended up fighting."

"For real, what's that kid name who got slashed on the back of his neck? To this day he don't know it was Butta who slashed him," Tre said.

"Word. Po po came and shut down the movies that night."

"All A.J. could do was beef that his new kicks got dirty," Ro said with a laugh.

Ro flipped through the rest of A.J.'s album, he saw several pictures of A.J. while he was younger and to his surprise a few of himself playing in some games. He closed the book and put it on the bed but not before taking the crew picture out of its pocket and placing it in his own pants pocket. Tre had stood up and was now looking through A.J.'s mixed tapes. Ro picked up A.J.'s ball that was lying next to his bed and held it tight. He then bounced it a few times. Just then A.J.'s two-year-old brother Victor walked into the room. He looked at Romelo then held both his little arms out.

"A…A…" he said while letting the pacifier fall from his mouth.

"What's up little Vic?" Butta asked.

He ignored everything and everybody except Ro and the ball.

"A," he said again, then began to cry.

"You want the ball Vic?" Ro asked him.

Mrs. Jimenez walked into the room and picked Victor up.

"He's trying to say Angel…Romelo you can have dat ball if you like. Yall take whatever yall want…what else am I gonna do with all his stuff?"

Mrs. Jimenez briskly walked out of the room holding Victor who was still crying and yelling for his brother. Romelo put the ball down on A.J.'s bed.

"Let's roll yall."

"Hol up, he got some tims in here," Lil Mickey said.

"Nigga come on, leave his stuff alone," Butta, uttered.

They said their goodbyes and headed for the door. As they were leaving they could hear Mrs. Jimenez yelling from the kitchen.

"MY ANGEL!!! LORD WHY MY ANGEL?"

They stepped out of apartment 9a.

In the staircase Nature and the rest were still drinking and smoking. Butta walked straight to Rugged and held his hand out. Rugged gave him the half empty vodka bottle. He put the bottle to his lips and drank hard. His face twisted up for a few seconds, "Whew," he blew out. He then passed the bottle to Romelo, and Ro did the same. Only instead of taking one long swig, he took three. He sat on the empty step right above Nature. A blunt made its way to Romelo. He took it and immediately pulled on it. Nature watched as Ro's eyes filled up with tears.

Nature smiled," that's some good shit right?" he asked.

Romelo nodded at his brother, but little did Nature know, those tears had nothing to do with the quality of the weed.

"So when we gon do this?" Tre asked.

"Tomorrow," Rugged answered.

"Yea...tomorrow," Lil Mickey repeated.

"Every other Saturday they work out at Calvin's crib, in the backyard. All dem niggas be there."

"You sure?" Tre asked while drinking from the bottle.

"Yea, I'm sure"

Romelo was beginning to feel the effects of the weed and vodka. He put his head down and rests it on his knees. He tried to concentrate on the conversation that was taking place but his mind kept drifting to Jada. Someone nudged him and when he lifted his head all he saw was the liquor bottle. He grabbed it and took another swig.

"Who all going?" Nature asked.

Romelo kept hearing Jada tell him that she loves him.

"Ro?" Butta yelled. Romelo lifted his head.

"Ro? Tomorrow son, dem niggas gonna pay!" Butta said angrily.

"Uh huh," Ro mumbled. "Tomorrow…yall know what? I'm a get married."

Everyone broke out in laughter.

"He gone…he fucked up," Nature said.

"Yea…tomorrow," Romelo mumbled.

They sat in the staircase for another forty minutes, mapping out a plan. The plans included Romelo and the death of Calvin. By the time they were ready to leave, Ro had to practically be carried home. He fell asleep on his bed with thoughts of Jada on his mind.

SATURDAY MORNING-JADA

Jada woke to the sounds of HOT97 FM. She had set her radio alarm clock to 7:00am. When she sat up she glanced at the clock.

"I'm 16," she said out loud. She then smiled ear to ear and got out of bed. Jada knew she had a lot to do today so she sat down, grabbed a piece of paper and a pencil and made a list.

THINGS TO DO TODAY
Wake up Monie
1. Go pick up our dresses.
2. Go get our hair done.
3. Go with mommy to center and finish decorating.
4. Go home and get ready.
5. Call daddy, see if he is coming???
6. Go to center and PARTY PARTY PARTY!!
7. Have Monie look out for Ro.
8. Send mommy home afterwards, clean up.
9. Chill with my baby.

"Hmmm, maybe I should make number 10 get married," Jada said.

She wrote it down on the pad and read it aloud over and over again.

"I'm so stupid," she said with a laugh. "But when? Maybe Monday…maybe Tuesday?"

She spun around in her seat. She reached for the phone and was getting ready to call Romelo when it rang.

"Hello?" she answered.

"Happy Birthday baby gurl."

"Oh…thank you Cancer."

"No prob. I got your gift, when's a good time to drop it off to you?"

"Cancer you didn't have to…"

"I know I didn't, but I did. When you want me to roll thru and bring it to you?" he asked.

"Well, i'm just about to go get Monie, how bout later?"

"Ok. When at the party?"

"Damn!" Jada thought. What could she tell him? Some sort of lie, because she really didn't want Cancer to come and ruin her night.

"Think Jay think."

"Hello?" Cancer said into the phone.

"Oh dang Cancer, I forgot to tell you. I decided to not have it."

"For real?" he asked skeptically.

"Yea, too much hassle. So me and Monie just gon go to the movies, maybe go out to eat," she lied.

"You been talking bout this for a minute now. So you just decided to not have it?"

"Yea…I'm saying, I'd rather just chill with my best friend. Turning 16 is no biggie."

"Aiight…well i'm a drop this off at your crib lata."

"Ok, that's cool…that's good," she said nervously.

"Aight, lata Jay."

"Later," she replied. Jada hung up the phone. She knew Cancer didn't believe a word she just said but she couldn't worry about him now, she had too much other stuff to think about, and to do. She picked the phone back up and dialed Romelo's number. She let the phone ring three times and was about to hang up when someone finally answered.

"Yea?" Nature said.

Music was blasting in the background so loud that Jay could hardly hear when Nature responded.

"Yea?" he said again.

"Hi, can I speak with Romelo?" she yelled.

"Who this?"

"This is Jada," she answered.

"Oh Jada...Ro is still sleep. I'll tell him you called."

Before Jay could reply she heard the dial tone. She figured she would just give him a call later. She quickly showered dressed and called Monica. They decided to meet at the train station and head to Lola's boutique in Manhattan. Once on the Manhattan bound 2 train, both girls sat down and giggled.

"Gurl I can't believe you 16 and you making plans on getting married," Monica squealed.

"Shhh," Jada said while looking around the practically empty train car.

"What? We don't know none of these people," Monica said while eyeing a man sitting across from them fast asleep with his baseball cap pulled down way below his eyes.

"I know right? It's just that i'm so nervous Monie.

Jada kept folding her hands in her lap then wringing them, and then folding them again. Monica looked at her best friend and grabbed her hands.

"Jay…you sure you want to do this?" she asked while looking in Jada's eyes.

Jada looked at Monica and squeezed her hands tight.

"I'm sure Monica…I…I know this all seems crazy and like a dream but I love him, I really do."

"Alright then boo boo, ohhhhhh I'm hatin on you right now. I want a Romeo!"

"You'll find one someday, maybe when you get older."

Monica looked at Jay and they burst out laughing.

"You only got me by a couple of months Jay, so don't even.

They rode the rest of their ride laughing, hugging and giggling. They exited the train station at Lexington Avenue and found Lola's boutique not too far from the station. Jada rang the bell outside the door.

"We have to be buzzed in," she explained.

"Ooh okay, dang your moms must have paid a lot for these dresses."

"I don't know, she hasn't told me the price. I think she got the hookup from a co-worker. But wait till you see yours Monie."

A saleswoman with shoulder length blonde hair, squared shaped glasses that sat on her forehead and a tape measure around her neck answered the door.

"Hi ladies, do you have an appointment?" she asked with a smile.

"Hi, yes i'm Jada Romain, here to pick up two dresses."

"Romain? Oh ok, we were expecting you yesterday Mrs. Romain," she said while opening the door and letting them in.

"I know, i'm sorry I got held up."

"Ummm hmmm," Monica chimed in with.

"Ok well i'm Anya and the dresses are over here."

They followed Anya to a huge glass table that was in the middle of the store. Dresses and material were scattered everywhere. Some hung on racks others laid across the backs of chairs or sofas.

"Have a seat ladies, I shall return."

Monica and Jada were to excited to sit down; Monica spotted a white wedding gown and ran to it.

"Jay! Look at this!" she half whispered, half yelled.

Jada turned around and her mouth hung open.

"Oh my God!" she said. "This is so beautiful."

"For real," Monica said. She then turned over the price tag that swung from the right sleeve.

"Lawd!"

"Is it bad?" Jay asked.

"Bad aint the word."

Jay stood back and admired the long gown. She lightly touched its lace fabric and smiled at what appeared to be tiny little pearls that hung on it. She refused to look at the price tag, didn't want to ruin her fantasy. Anya came over and interrupted by clearing her throat politely.

"Here we go ladies," she said.

She unzipped the garment bag and pulled out Jada's dress. Both girls stared in amazement. Jada grabbed the dress and ran to the fitting room.

"Let me try it on. Monie try yours also!"

Jada changed quickly and stepped out to view herself in the full-length mirror. She wore a cream colored silk dress with spaghetti straps. It was form fitting down to the waist then it flared out and covered her feet. The back was a little longer then the front, it gave off the image of a small train behind her. She stared at her own reflection in the mirror.

"Wait till Ro sees me in this," she thought.

Monica peeked out the dressing room and saw Jada.

"Oh my God Jay!" she said while holding the dressing room doors open. "You look amazing."

"Thanks Monie. Come out let me see. Does it fit?"

Jada's mother had chosen a burgundy satin dress for Monica. It had a look similar to Jada's dress only it wasn't as long and it had a lower neckline.

"How I look?" Monica asked while stepping in front of the mirror.

"Gurl I didn't know you had breastessesss" Jada joked.

I didn't either," Monica replied.

"You look beautiful Monie."

"Yes you do, both you ladies do," Anya said. "That dress is made to uplift you in the front, giving you a more…how can I say? Healthier appearance."

"Do I look too healthy?

"No, you so silly Monie."

"So everything is to your liking Mrs. Romain"

"Yes it is Anya, thank you so much."

"I'm glad. Now if you ladies please take them off, I can go ahead and wrap them up for you."

"Ok," they answered in unison.

"Man Monie, I wouldn't mind getting married in this dress here. You think Ro would like this?"

"Of course…hey Jay? When yall getting married? And afterwards, where are yall gonna live?"

Jada reached over to Monica and helped her unzip.

"Well were going to continue to live at home. Him with his family and me with my mother. That's until we finish high school and were gonna both apply to the same college. Once in college we will live together off campus somewhere. In the meantime between school and basketball, he's gonna get a job, and i'm going to try to find something after school and were gonna start saving money. As for the when? I don't know…maybe tomorrow, Monday…next week."

Monica stepped out of her dress and handed it to Anya. She then looked at her best friend. "Dang it seems like yall got it all worked out. Yall ain't playing huh? Shoot I ain't mad atcha. I still say yall are crazy tho."

"Not crazy Monie, just in love."

Monica went back into the dressing room to change while Jay admired herself in the mirror a lil while longer.

"Jada Jones," she said aloud, and then broke out into a huge smile.

ROMELO

Romelo woke to the sounds of the Notorious B.I.G. "I love it when they call me big poppa…" He opened one eye and for a second he couldn't figure out where he was. His head was pounding, his stomach was feeling nauseous and he felt as if he was about to vomit. When he finally managed to get the other eye opened, he recognized his own room. He glanced at his radio, which sat, atop his dresser. The bass from the radio was causing some of his basketball trophies to rattle. He squeezed his eyes shut for a second then opened them again. This time he noticed Butta going through his closet. He sat up and his nostrils were automatically hit with the worse stench had ever smelled. He looked down and realized he was still wearing the outfit he had on yesterday. Only difference was that there was a pink sort of cottage cheese looking substance stuck to the front of his hoodie. He quickly realized that was where the smell was coming from. Romelo began to take off his hoodie when Nature walked in with a lit blunt in his hand. The refer smell made him feel even worse.

"Yo you find something?" he asked Butta.

"What chall looking for?" Romelo asked.

"Oh you up. Butta needs a black shirt or hoodie or somethang."

"Yea i'm up…I feel like i'm about to call earl tho. Why yall let me sleep in this shit?"

Both Butta and Nature laughed.

"Damn nigga, I ain't know you threw up on yourself," Butta said while still laughing. Romelo lifted the hoodie over his head carefully, trying not to get any of the vomit on his face or stocking cap. Once he had it off he threw it at Butta.

"Yo chill!" Butta yelled while dodging it.

Ro tried to stand up; he became lightheaded when he did so he quickly sat back down.

"Damn, I think i'm gon throw up again."

"Only one way to feel better from a hang ova. And that's to get high all over again," Nature said while sitting down on the bed next to Ro.

"For real, I woke up feeling like shit also but two puffs lata, i'm a new man," Butta said.

Ro and Nature laughed.

"Shut up Butta man, you'se a fool."

Tre walked into the room with two brown paper bags under each arm and with Lil Mickey trailing him.

"Ewww, what's dat smell?"

"Yo moms was just in here," Nature said.

"Ro threw up on his self," Butta answered.

"Baby! Here drink some of this."

Tre passed a 40-ounce of beer to Ro.

"Beer in the morning is supposed to make me feel better?"

"Its afternoon nigga," Nature said while taking the other bottle of beer from Tre. He took a long swig then got up from the bed. When he turned the radio back up again the trophies began to shake. Lil Mickey held his hand up to Nature.

"Pass the brew kid."

"When you grow," Nature joked.

"I'm big enough for your grandma," he said while clutching the front of his jeans.

"Ooohh," Butta and Tre said.

"What?" Nature asked. He grabbed Lil Mickey and threw him on the bed next to Ro. He sat on Lil Mickey's chest and punched him in the stomach.

"Ahhhh!" Lil Mickey screamed out.

"Yo past me that shit with the vomit on it!"

"No!! Chill man. I'm sorry!"

"Yall gon make me throw up again if you bring that hoodie over here," Ro said while watching Nature and Lil Mickey.

Butta passed the blunt to Ro and he passed it right on to Tre. He laid his head down on the pillow and prayed for his nausea to go away.

"The phone ringing!"Butta yelled.

"You lucky," Nature said while getting up off of Lil Mickey's chest. He went into the kitchen to answer the phone. Ro grabbed the 40oz. And drank some more, hoping what Butta and Nature said was true.

When Nature came back in the room, Ro asked him who was it on the phone.

"Nobody yo," he replied.

Just then Rugged walked into the bedroom with two large green duffle bags.

"Aight girls, this is where the fun begins. These shits right here, are strictly on loan from Black Dread. Wait, where's gammy and Nae?"

"Nae took gammy out to IHOP," Nature replied.

Rugged placed the bags carefully down on Ro's bed.

"Lemme see," said and excited Lil Mickey.

Rugged unzipped the larger of the two bags. He reached in and pulled out an AK-47.

"Got damn! I knew Black Dread was gonna come thru, you was right Rugged, he must have owed you big time," Nature said.

Romelo looked over to see what all the fuss was about. When he saw the weapon in Lil Mickey's hand, bits and pieces of last nights conversation flooded his head. He remembered something about Calvin lifting weight every Saturday. The phone rang again and Nature ran out the room. Butta turned up the volume on Ro's radio. Blunts, beer and guns were being passed around like groupies at an after party. Romelo sat back on his bed and held his head.

"I can't do this," he said aloud.

"Huh?" Rugged asked.

Romelo stood up, feeling a little light headed, he steadied himself then repeated what he had just said. Nature walked back into the room.

"Bitch been callin here all day!"

Ro looked at Nature. "Who? Jay? Did she call?"

"Naw. I was talking bout somebody else," Nature lied.

He knew if he gave Ro the phone, Jada was going to talk him out of it or discourage him from even going along on the ride. So for the fourth time today he told Jay that Ro was still asleep and he assured her that he would tell Ro that she had called soon as he woke. Ro's stomach felt queasy so he sat back down on the bed. He took the blunt from Rugged and pulled. In between exhales he thought of ways he could get out of this, but deep down inside he knew he couldn't. Someone had started an A.J. story and the whole room was listening. Some of them nodded in agreement when Tre announced that, "This shit has got to end." The more they talked about Vector houses and Cancer and his crew, the more riled up they became.

Ro remained pensive. He thought about what he had planned for Jada tonight. Some candles, borrow a twenty spot from Rugged to get her some roses, read her the poem he wrote for her, and just get lost in her presence. Ro was jolted from these thoughts when Lil Mickey plopped down on the bed beside him with a tech 9 in his hand.

"Sup Lil Mickey?" he asked him.

"Not a damn thang. Ain't this shit pretty?" he asked while holding up the nine.

"Get that thing away from me," Ro said.

Lil Mickey sucked his teeth then placed the nine down on the bed beside him.

"It ain't loaded man. But I can't wait to add to it. Can't wait to pump some family enders. I'm aiming straight for Calvin then Rayson. And who ever get caught in between, then that's their bad."

Ro rubbed his forehead then looked at Lil Mickey. He noticed him wiping tears from his eyes.

"You alright?"

"Yea man...it's just that I loved A.J. that was my dawg. Nawimean? I got love for all yall and would die for yall niggas any day, yall my fam..."

Ro knew there was no way of getting out of this now. He felt like he owed it to A.J. owed it to everybody in this room. The plans he had with Jada would still take place; He knew he had the rest of his life with her. But for now, at this very moment, as Nature would say, it was strictly crew love.

CANCER

Cancer got off the phone with Jada feeling uneasy. He didn't know whether to believe her or not. She had been planning this party for sometime and all of a sudden, it's no biggie?

"Fuck it," he said out loud. He decided he was going to give her the benefit of the doubt even though he felt she didn't deserve it. "Baby gurl been slipping lately," he thought. But its ok after giving her, her gift it's gonna be all good. Cancer figured he had been waiting for this moment for about four years now. And he couldn't wait any longer. Couldn't wait to tell Jada that he was in love with her. Has been since she was eleven years old. He was ready for her to be his. He pulled the small velvet burgundy box out of his pants pocket. He opened it up and smiled at the diamond that seemed to be smiling back at him.

"Happy Birthday baby gurl," he practiced.

He decided, after looking at his reflection in the mirror, to go get a haircut, then hookup with Jules. Go check on Calvin and them and then later on tonight give Jada her gift. He closed the box and put it back in his pocket.

JADA

Once Jay and Monie were finished getting their hair done, they eyed themselves in the mirror. Jada had her hair swept up into a French twist; she had Monique add some baby breaths to the back of the twist. Monica decided to take her braids out and went for a simple wrap. She had Monique leave the bobby pins in. Both girls stepped outside the salon and immediately tied a scarf around their heads. Jada looked at her watch.

"Dang I can't believe how fast this day is going. I wish it would slow down."

"Word," said Monie. "You only hit 16 once in your life."

They walked to the train station and rode back to the Bronx.

Once they were back in Vector, Monica decided to head to the center to see if her help was needed in the decorating.

"They should be finished by now but I want to see how it looks."

"My moms and yours? Working together? Oh yeah, they hooked it up," Jay said with a smile.

"Alright girl, I'm a see you in a lil while." Monica leaned into Jada and gave her a big hug.

"Thanks girl. Thanks for paying to get my hair done.'

"No problem Jay. You my gurl! Sides what can you get someone who already has errythang?"

141

"No, I don't have everything but come tomorrow I will be one step closer to it."

Both girls said their see you lata's and Jay headed home. She was so glad that the day turned out to be beautiful. She looked up at the sky and smiled. It was bright, sunny, not too cold and not too hot. A perfect September afternoon she thought. Jay knew she had never been this happy in her life. Not even Cancer catching her in a lie was going to ruin her mood. When she reached her house she noticed an unfamiliar car parked in the driveway. She didn't see her mother's car so she figured her moms was still at the center. Jay unlocked the front door and headed straight upstairs to her bedroom. She carefully laid her dress across the chair then plopped down onto her bed. Something soft fell down onto Jay's face and she sat up quickly. It was a huge Winnie the Pooh stuffed animal with a card fixed between its two paws.

"Awww, Winnie!"

She pulled the card from between Winnie's paws and saw something shiny hanging on him. Upon closer inspection Jada realized that Winnie had a tennis bracelet around his wrist. She squealed in delight. She quickly undid the latch and ran to her dresser mirror. She put it around her wrist and fastened it. "It's so pretty," she said aloud. Jada then reached for the card and opened it. She read Hallmarks words then read the words that were written in black ink.

"To Jada, I can't believe your already 16. You're still my little girl. Miss you dearly, love you much." And it was signed, "Daddy."

Jada touched the bracelet with her left hand as she read the card again. She sat down on her bed, grabbed Winnie and held him tight. The clock in Jada's room struck four.

"Dang, I have just about an hour till my party begins."

Jay decided to try Romelo once more. She picked up the phone and dialed. She prayed Nature didn't answer the phone like he has been doing all day. She had a feeling Nature didn't like her and was lying to her about Romelo's whereabouts.

"Hello?" a voice answered.

"Yes! It's gammy," Jay thought.

"Hi Mrs. Brooks. Is Romelo home?"

"No honey, Romelo stepped out."

"Oh ok. Could your tell him that Jada called and I said I will see him tonight at our spot."

"Ok, I will honey, I sure will."

Jada put the phone down on its cradle and went to run her bath. Once the water was at a comfortable enough temperature, Jada got in, sank deep down and closed her eyes. Her thoughts played a ping-pong match in her head. From Romelo to her father and back again.

ROMELO

"Man…what time is it?"

"It's four o'clock."

"We been sitting here for nearly two hours and Butta's been gone for almost thirty." Lil Mickey said.

"I know, I know…he'll be back soon. Let's go ova this again," Ro said to no one in particular.

Tre and Lil Mickey both shot Ro a look of disbelief.

"Ro! We don't need to go over this again aight? We got it. All we need is for Butta to bring his ass on. Its gon start getting dark soon."

"What? You afraid of the dark nigga?" Lil Mickey asked Tre.

"No, not one of us has a driver's license fool! And i'm not bout to be pulled ova. I'm not tryna see the inside of no ones central booking." Tre opened the car door on the stolen red Honda and got out.

"I need to stretch my fuckin legs." Ro watched Tre walk around the Honda then lean against the hood.

"Damn! Where is Butta?" Lil Mickey asked.

Romelo didn't even acknowledge Lil Mickey, instead he thought of Jada and how he was going to be with his baby later tonight. He wondered what she was doing now, probably her hair or something like that. He hoped that she didn't mind that he didn't get her anything; he definitely planned on making that up to her.

"…Probably tryna holla at some gurl, knowing Butta…" Lil Mickey's words bought Romelo back to the business at hand. Tre stepped on the Newport he had been puffing on and got back in the driver's seat.

"Here he comes," Tre announced.

Lil Mickey perked up, "Where?"

Tre pointed and all three of them looked up the block. Butta was trotting toward the car. He had his dreads pulled back into a tight ponytail and had a black knit cap over them. Butta's attire was all black as were everyone else's. As Butta approached the car, he began to walk. Across the street, two young guys were walking and watching Butta. Butta pulled his hat down farther and glanced in their direction. He tried to make out who they were as they did him. One of the cats threw his two fingers up in the air.

"What up son?" he yelled to Butta.

"Sup?" Butta yelled back.

He approached the car slowly and right before he opened the passenger door, he turned to see if they were looking. When he saw that they wasn't, he got in.

"Who was that? You know them?" Lil Mickey asked.

"No, I don't know who they were. Probably thought the knew me from round here."

"Oh…what took you so long?"

"Nobody told Tre to park so far away. Shit! I had to walk the two blocks, then another two. Come up around Trade so that I was behind the house."

"So who all out there?" Ro asked. He and Tre had turned around in their seats and were now facing Butta and Lil Mickey who sat in the back seat.

"From what I could see, its Calvin of course, Rayson, Bilal, doo-rag, Shamar and a few other cats, I don't know they names."

"And they all in the back yard?" Tre asked.

"Yeah…Calvin was lifting weights. The rest was either shooting hoops or just sitting around."

"Yea…okay," Lil Mickey said.

Romelo turned back around to face front. He looked up the street then at the dashboard clock; the time read 4:39 p.m.

"Tre, you keep the doors open and the motor running."

"I know Ro."

"Lil Mickey and Butta you come with me. We go inside the fence, Butta you stand in front of the house. Lil Mickey and myself will go down that small path to the back of the house…"

"I got Calvin yo! I got his ass!" Lil Mickey said excitedly.

"Aight Lil Mickey…and I got your back."

Ro secretly wished he could get out of this but he knew he couldn't. He looked up at the sky and thought how beautiful it looked, velvet skies. He gazed at the almost perfect cloud formations and wished he could be sitting on one of them clouds right about now.

"What chu looking at Ro?" Butta asked.

"The sky…it's a perfect day."

"Yea, a perfect day to die."

Ro looked at Tre, then at Butta and finally Lil Mickey. He looked back up at the sky and said, "Let's get this shit over with."

Tre took the Honda out of park and drove the two and a half blocks to Trade. No one uttered a word until he pulled up in front of house 1680. Romelo glanced over at Calvin's mother's house then at Tre. Tre looked in the rear view mirror then back at Romelo and nodded. Romelo got out of the car first and pulled the hood to his black Champion sweatshirt over his head. He reached in the car, opened the glove compartment and pulled out the .45 glock Rugged had given him earlier. He looked at Butta and Lil Mickey and said, "let's go yall." Butta put his black knit cap back on and tied a black handkerchief around his nose and mouth. Lil Mickey did the same, then pulled his hood over his head. Both guys got out the car and walked over to Romelo who was feeling nervous because he had left his handkerchief at home. He pulled the draw stings as far as he could until the only visible features of his face were his nose and eyes. After Lil Mickey retrieved his and Butta's weapons from out of the trunk, all three walked towards the house, Lil Mickey lifted the latch on the fence and let them in. Butta stood in the front yard, AK47 in hand, Lil Mickey led Ro down the narrow path to the back of the house.

They could hear music and people talking. Romelo pulled the strings to his sweat hood again; he then put his hand over his heart. His heart was beating so hard he thought any minute now it was gonna break a hole in his chest. Lil Mickey stopped at the edge of the pathway and peeked around the corner. He turned back to see if Butta was still at the front; he was.

"Let's do this!"

Lil Mickey took off running, he ran around the corner to the back yard, yelling the whole time.

"YEAAAAAHHHHHH!!!!"

Ro ran behind him. He stopped right next to him, aimed his 45 towards the top of the trees and began squeezing the trigger.

Everyone in Calvin's Mother's back yard hit the ground. Lil Mickey aimed the shottie towards Calvin who was lying on the weight bench. Calvin looked in the direction of the gunmen and quickly rolled off the bench landing face first onto the ground. Lil Mickey pumped then pulled the trigger. He blasted a hole in the fence, missing Calvin by an inch or two.

"Mutha fucka!" Calvin yelled.

Lil Mickey pumped again and looked at a frightened Calvin who was trying to crawl underneath the weight bench. Just then the back door to the house opened up and Calvin's mother stepped out.

"What's going…"

Thinking it was another one of Calvin's boys; Lil Mickey quickly aimed for the figure at the back door and pulled the trigger again.

Mrs. Harris fell to the ground.

Ro stared in disbelief, suddenly he felt something fly by his face, and he looked to his right and saw Rayson aiming a gun at him. He turned his gun to Rayson and squeezed. He missed and yelled to Lil Mickey.

"Let's go!"

Someone else began shooting at them as well, they headed towards the stolen car. Calvin reached for his gun and scrambled to his feet. He looked at his mother, who was lying in a pool of her own blood and yelled. "Git dem bitches!"

At least five of them ran after Romelo and Lil Mickey, with Calvin leading the pack. He aimed for them and began shooting. Butta and Tre heard the shooting as it got louder and seemed to be coming in their direction. Tre sat up straight and squeezed the steering wheel.

"Come on yall," he whispered over and over again.

Butta aimed the AK in the direction of the noise; he watched Ro and Lil Mickey as they flew past him.

"Come on!" Ro yelled to him.

Calvin emerged right behind Lil Mickey; he looked at Butta who stood looking at him. He watched in what seemed to be slow motion as Butta raised his weapon and fired. The bullets caught Calvin in the side causing him to fall over and land in his mother's flowerbed. Rayson and the rest, who were following Calvin, hit the ground in cover. Ro, Lil Mickey and Butta jumped into the car and Tre pulled off, not even giving them enough time to close the doors.

"Oh shit…oh shit…oh shit!" Butta kept repeating over and over again.

"Where am I going?" Tre asked nervously.

Oh shit!" Butta said again.

Ro pulled the hood off his head and looked at the passenger side mirror.

"Where am I going??!!" Tre yelled.

"Manhattan, let's dump it in Manhattan," Ro said while still looking at the mirror. "And slow down Tre, we don't wanna get pulled over."

Ro felt the pressure on his chest lift somewhat. But he couldn't take his eyes off the mirror. He thought he heard the unmistakable sounds of a police siren some where off in the distance.

"Come on Tre, move this bitch."

"You just told me to slow down!" Tre yelled.

"Where in Manhattan?"

"I don't know man! The village, some where…I don't care."

"Oh shit," Butta said again.

"Butta! What da fuck?" Ro turned to face Butta and looked at Lil Mickey. Lil Mickey sat slanted, he was leaning his head on the window and had his eyes closed.

"Mickey?" Ro yelled.

Butta turned to look at Mickey then yelled his name as well.

"Mickey!"

"What?" Tre asked nervously, eyes moving from the street to the rearview and back again. Butta nudged him on his arm and Lil Mickey opened his eyes.

"What's wrong wit you?" Butta asked.

"What?" Tre asked again.

Lil Mickey pulled his hands from under his jacket and looked down at his palms. They were covered in blood.

"Oh shit!" Butta yelled.

"Oh shit!" yelled Ro.

"What, shit?" Tre asked, straining to see in the rear view mirror.

"I think I got hit" Lil Mickey said, his voice trembling.

"What we gon do?" Tre asked.

Butta reached over and lifted Lil Mickey's jacket. His shirt was soaked in blood; he then lifted the shirt and saw a dark red hole that was about the size of a quarter. Butta pulled the shirt back down and looked at Romelo.

"Oh dang nigga that ain't nuthin," Ro said to Lil Mickey.

"No? It doesn't look bad?" Mickey said while looking Ro in the eyes.

"Hell no, "Butta said, feeding off of Ro's vibe.

"Just look like a flesh wound. Chill son we got you."

"What da fuck we gonna do?" Tre asked.

"Take him to a hospital, what else?" replied Butta.

"Shit no!" Tre said.

"What just drop him off? Cause we can't all go in there with him."

"Yall just drop me off...yall know I got c'halls back," Lil Mickey said. He then coughed and let out a low moan. Ro punched the car's dashboard.

"Shit!" he yelled and punched it again.

"Turn around," he said calmly.

"What?"

"Turn around. Foster...Nature will know what to do."

JADA

Monica and her mother came to pick Jay up at 5:45 p.m. Jada stepped out of her house and smiled at them both. Monica got out the car and ran up to her best friend.

"Ooh you look sooo beautiful," she said to Jay while giving her a big hug.

"Thank you boo boo, you do too. Your hair is tight!"

"Ma! Come here," Monie yelled to her mother.

"Take our picture!" Monica's mother was already headed towards the girl, camera in hand.

"Wait...hold up. What's that on your wrist?" Monie asked, eyes glued to Jada's new tennis bracelet.

"Oh yea look Monie! Guess who gave it to me?"

"Who? Romeo?"

"Nope, my dad."

"Say word...where is he? Is he here?"

"I haven't seen him, I think he mailed it and my moms put it on my bed with this huge Winnie the Pooh."

"You and your Winnie," Monie said with a laugh.

"Say cheese!" Monica's mother instructed. Both girls cheesed for the camera.

"Where's your moms? She ready?"

"She's in the shower. She said she would meet us there in a few. I haven't really seen her all day. She has been running in and out. Acting all secretive. I don't know what's up. But it better be good."

They posed for two more pictures, and then headed to the center. Jada arrived at the center just as the sun was setting. She viewed the sky and imagined this is what Romelo would call "velvet skies." She wondered where he was and couldn't wait until they met again tonight.

Her and Monica stepped into the room, her mother had rented out and was automatically greeted by a few partygoers.

"Sup Jay, happy birthday!" said Mona.

"Happy birthday gurl, you look beautiful," chimed in Melissa.

Mr. Moe, who used to cut Terrance hair when he was a little boy, gave her a hug and held on tight. A little too tight for Jay.

"Gurl you looking as good as your momma."

It was apparent to Jay by the smell of liquor on Mr. Moe's breath that he had started partying a whole lot earlier today.

"Speaking of yo momma, there she is."

Jada turned to look in the direction Mr. Moe was facing and saw her mother enter the room with a man trailing her. Because the DJ had already dimmed the lights, Jay squinted to see who this person was approaching her along with her mother. As he got closer, Jada's eyes opened wide.

"DADDY?"

Reggie Romain leaned into his daughter and took her in his arms.

"Hey baby gurl...ummmm," he said while squeezing her tight.

"Daddy!" she said with glee.

153

He pulled her away from him and stared at her face.

"Happy Birthday Jada," He said.

Jada watched as a single tear rolled down his cheek.

"Aww daddy, don't do that. You gonna make me cry. And you know I'm not tryna have no tears at my party."

"Okay…okay," he said while swiping at his cheek.

They both turned to look at Jada's mother who was standing there watching them both joyfully.

"Come here Jay, gimmie hug," Mary said.

"Hey mommy." Jada flew into her mother's arms.

"Where have you been all day?"

"Shoot girl, it was hard tryna keep this man hidden from you. We both wanted to surprise you."

"Thank you mommy," Jay said and she kissed her mother on the cheek.

"I see you got your gift," Reggie said while admiring the bracelet.

"Oh yes, its beautiful daddy. How did you know I wanted one?"

"Your mother told me."

Jada watched her father smile at her mother and her moms look away embarrassed.

"Umm, is there something yall wanna tell me?" Jay said with a smile.

"We can talk lata. Right now I want to dance with the birthday girl. You think the DJ can play something from my generation?"

"Daddy this is Jay-z anyone can bounce to Jay-z."

She grabbed his hand and led him to the dance floor. Jada stayed on the floor practically the whole night. She danced with her father several times, her mother, Monica and practically every guy in there. She only stopped once and that was in order to chow down on some honey barbecue chicken wings and potato salad, courtesy of Monica's mother. She looked around the room and noticed how packed the gift table had gotten. She decided she would open them later on tonight. Jada was more then happy to see that Calvin or none of his friends showed up, and for a second her thoughts drifted to Cancer, with the way he had been acting lately, she hoped he didn't try to come over tonight. The DJ slowed things down a little bit by putting on Aaliyah's, One in a million. Since Ro wasn't there to dance with, Jay grabbed the hand of the only other man in her life that she loved.

"Come on daddy."

They found a spot on the floor and began to dance to the beat.

"So, how's North Carolina?" she asked.

"It's fine...kinda slow. Not at all like New York. Nothings like New York. But I like it."

"So you and mom? What's up?"

Reggie looked over at Mary who was sitting watching them.

"Well baby were talking...a lot of talking. But that's a beginning right?"

"Right...don't you ever miss us daddy?"

"Ofcourse I do. You know I still love your mother and you very very much, yall are all I think about." He hugged his daughter tight.

"But I don't miss that!" he said while the sounds of an ambulance could be heard coming from outside. Later on that night Jay and Monica had a chance to talk alone in the ladies room. While Jada wiped the sweat off her forehead, Monica applied a fresh coat of lip-gloss to her lips.

"Dang! It is hot in there," Jay said while fanning herself.

"That's not the only hot spot. Man the block is on fire! Have you heard all those sirens? Ambulance, po po, I wonder what happened? And I haven't seen Romeo no where in sight."

"Yea I heard them. I guess that's why he didn't show, to hot outside. I guess I will see him later on tonight, you still gonna drop me off right?"

"Yea while they cleaning up, I'm a take you."

CANCER

Cancer stepped out of Mako's Cuts feeling good. He had the little bit of hair on his head shaved. His baldhead glistened under the September sun. He rubbed his face; the new growth of whiskers was gone also. He reached in his pocket and pulled the diamond stud earring he had taken off earlier and put it back in his left ear. He caught his reflection in the bodega's window and smiled. He had just spent the last two hours in Mako's getting his head shaved, a facial, nails done and he even acquired two new customers for his booming street business. A chocolate colored female in a hunter green Ford Explorer, pulled up to the curb where Cancer was standing. She honked her horn and rolled down the passenger side window.

"Hey cancer, how you feel?" she said with a fuck me grin.

"I feel good as fuck dashaia," he replied.

"You look good enough to fuck too. What's up for the evening? What you got going on?"

"I got big plans girl...big plans."

He reached in his phat farm denim jacket and pulled out a small velvet box with the silver ribbon on it. He held up the box for dashaia to see.

"Damn! It's like dat? Keisha one lucky bitch."

"Keisha?" Cancer said with a laugh.

He laughed out loud all the way to his car He put the box back in his pocket and decided to stop by Calvin's crib before he went home and changed. He

157

glanced at his watch; it read 5:00 p.m. He wondered had Jada and Monica gone to the movies yet. He was glad she decided against the party, he didn't want a bunch of knuckleheads around when he gave her his gift anyway. Ever since he spoke to her earlier today, he imagined how the evening with her would go. He smiled at the thought of its outcome. Cancer got so caught up in his thoughts that he almost ran past a stop sign. The car making a left at the intersection honked its horn and reminded him where he was. He turned his car stereo on and pressed play. DMX growled and asked at a decibel of 10, 'where my dogs at?' He saw the light to his pager, which was lying on the dashboard blinking, but he figured it was Calvin, Tariq or a customer. Either way, he thought, they would have to wait. An ambulance sped past Cancer while he mouthed the words to DMX.

"What them niggas did now?" he asked out loud.

Cancer drove a few more blocks and noticed how many people were populating the next block, Calvin's block. A cop at the intersection forbid him from entering onto the street so he made a left on loud street and found a parking spot. He got out and looked up the block, police was everywhere, and yellow police tape acted as a barrier to the rest of Vector. Big Stan and Ramel walked up to Cancer and gave him a pound. Cancer looked around for Calvin but didn't see him.

"What happened?" he asked the duo.

"Shitttttttt! Hell if I know. All we heard so far is some niggas blew away Calvin and his whole family," Big Stan answered.

"What??" Cancer asked with nothing but shock in his voice.

"Yea, 5 oh came in and arrested whoever the hell else was left alive. Rayson was out there crying like a little bitch."

"They know who did it?"

"Naw, they say it was a bunch of niggas who rolled up to the house and ambushed them. Some stood in the front, some went around back. Bust in the house killed all them. Shit! Some ruthless niggas, maybe Calvin owed somebody," said Ramel.

"Calvin worked for me. Yall know that! He was strickly five dolla or ten dollas. Small time. He ain't owe nobody, his business was my business. This shit here was personal."

While talking to Big Stan and Ramel, Cancer spotted a cop who he had a working relationship with, someone who looked the other way when Cancer rolled through. Someone whose palm was greased in return for looking the other way. He walked over to the yellow police tape, lifted it up over his head and proceeded to head up the block. He headed towards officer friendly and nodded at him.

"Excuse me, you need to step back behind the yellow tape."

Officer friendly escorted Cancer back to the tape and they conversed in hushed tones.

"What's up yo?"

"Not good man, Calvin's dead. They blew a hole in him the size of a fuckin bowling ball. Killed his mother too."

"Yall know who did it?"

"Working on it...whoever they were, one of them was hit also. Forensic picked up blood near the curb. No where near Calvin or his mother. They will run test. We have witnesses, a vehicle, they left a trail a mile long behind them. Those assholes will be caught by daybreak. Believe me on that."

Officer Friendly lifted up the tape and Cancer crossed back under. He turned to face the cop.

"In your opinion? Who you think?"

"In my opinion…some little boy's tryna be men. Some little boys who might not live too far from here. Some little boys who might have wanted some sort of revenge."

Officer Friendly headed back towards the crime scene while Cancer headed towards his car.

"Some little boys," he said while sitting behind the wheel.

Police was everywhere; so Cancer decided to head on home, make a few phone calls and then shower and change. He pulled right and steered towards Carol Ave. He passed Thornwood first and did what had become regular routine for him. He glanced up the block towards Jada's house. When he spotted a vehicle pulling into the driveway of house 3210. Cancer quickly whipped around the block and pulled up in front of the Romain house. Reggie Romain was leaning against his gold sun fire, smoking a cigarette. He looked over at the vehicle and recognized his driver.

"Cancer?"

Cancer got out of the car and greeted Mr. Romain with a handshake.

"Hey Mr. Romain, man long time no see, he said.

"Cancer, man look at you!" Reggie said while shaking his hand.

"You getting big there son."

Mary Romain came out the front door with a smile.
"Ok, I'm finally ready. Oh hi Cancer."

"Hello Mrs. Romain," he said while eyeing her outfit.

Mrs. Romain wore a below the knee length, off white spaghetti strap dress. With a matching sheer shawl she had wrapped around her shoulders. And while Mr. Romain went to take the bag out of her hands, he noticed that Reggie also was dressed to impress.

"You look beautiful Mrs. Romain," he said.

"Thank you sweetie."

She got inside of the car and began to apply another coat of lipstick.

Mr. Romain took Cancer's hand again and shook it.

"It was nice seeing you again Cancer. Were gonna see you at the party right?"

"The party? Oh yea...yea I'll be there. No doubt, just need to go shower you know? Freshen up"

"Alright, see you later."

Cancer watched the sun fire as it pulled off; he followed it with his eyes as it went up the block and around the corner.

Cancer was furious; he turned and looked up to Jada's bedroom window.

"Bitch!" he said out loud.

"Fuckin tryna play me!"

He reached in his pocket and pulled out the small box again. Cancer let his fingers rub across the velvet, then he wrapped his fist around the tiny box and squeezed. He raised his fist behind his head and was ready to throw the box hard enough to break Jada's bedroom window. But he suddenly dropped his hand and put the box back in his pocket.

"I'm a see you lata," he thought and then got in his car to drive home.

ROMELO

Nae Nae was awakened from her nap on the couch by banging at the front door. She slowly got up and wobbled towards the noise.

"Who is it?" she asked while pressing her right eye up against the peephole.

"Open up Nae!" Romelo said hurriedly.

"What's up Ro? Why you banging…" before she could finish her question Ro pushed the door open and ran inside.

Nae Nae automatically spotted the blood on his hands and shirt.

"Oh my God Ro! What happened? You alright?"

"Where's Nature?" he asked while looking at Nae Nae with an expression of sheer fear.

"He's in the room with Rug baggin up." She looked at Ro's hands and then back at his face and called for her brother.

"Nature! Nature c'mere!"

Nature came out of the bedroom with shorts saggin to his knees and a cigarette dangling from his lips.

"What Nae?" Nature saw Ro standing next to her and then he saw the blood.

"What happened Ro?"

"Shit went all wrong Nature," Ro answered while pacing back and forth.

"You hit? Where everybody else at"?

Ro couldn't answer he just kept pacing and banging his fist on his thigh.

"Stop walking back and forth and answer me Ro!"

Rugged heard all the commotion and came into the living room.

"What happened man?"

"Mannnn, we waited for the right time, when they was all together and I left my scarf here and Butta took a long time to come back...me and Lil Mickey went around back and then niggas dropped to the ground. We ran and Butta blast Calvin...next thing we know Lil Mickey in the backseat bleeding..."

"What?" Rugged asked.

"Ro, please, you making me nervous. I need to sit down," Nae Nae said.

"Where's Lil Mickey now?" Nature asked.

"In the basement, downstairs."

"Yall bought him here?" Nature yelled.

"We didn't know what else to do man...we didn't know..."

"Oh my God, Is he dead?" Nae asked.

"No, he wasn't when I left them."

"Okay, hold up, let me think."

All three of them watched while Nature took a long pull off of his cigarette.

"Alright, we gon dump him somewhere, call an ambulance, let them come get him. He's not gonna start singing is he?"

"No, no phone calls from here. No connections," Rugged said.

"I'm...I'm not dumping him Nature. That's my man. I'm not leaving him. And no he's not gonna say shit to the police." Ro said through pressed teeth.

"Well then how the fuck is he gonna get to a hospital?"

"I will fuckin carry him and walk if I have to! He wouldn't leave me if it was me and you know you wouldn't leave Rugged if it was him."

Rugged and Nature exchanged looks, they both knew what Ro just said was true.

"Ok, we will drive him. I want the rest of them niggas to go home and just stay there…we'll drop him off Ro, at emergency and that's it. Yall gonna need to lay low, maybe go stay wit Uncle Lincoln and them in Jersey."

"No cause if they start missing school, its gonna look suspicious," Nae Nae said.

"True…true," Rugged added.

"Shit! Jada!" Romelo said while smacking his forehead.

"Jada? What? What the fuck does she hafta do with any of this," Nature asked.

"It's her birthday today; I was posed to meet her on the roof tonight. Nature I need you to go to her…tell her I'm sorry, tell her what happened, and tell her I love her. And if I have to leave New York I want her to come with me."

"Ro this ain't the time for this bullshit," Nature started.

"It's not bullshit Nature, please!" Ro yelled. He didn't even bother to stop the tear from escaping and flowing down his cheek.

"I'm not gonna dump Lil Mickey, you can just drop us off at the hospital but i'm staying just till I know he's gonna be alright. But Nature please…please go to the roof for me."

"She means that much to you Romelo?"

"Yea man."

"Aight Ro, me and Nature is gonna drop you and Lil Mickey at the emergency. I'm gon stay with you and Nature is gonna come back and go to the roof and get Jada, right Nature?" Rugged asked.

Nature sucked his teeth and looked at his younger brother.

"Yea aight. Nae Nae you stay here, keep an eye out on the home front and gammy. Let me go put something on my feet then we out."

Nature quickly threw on some sweats and his timbs; they headed to the basement and found Butta and Tre sitting on the ground a few feet away from Lil Mickey. Nature and Rugged went straight to him and checked his wound. Romelo looked at Butta and Tre and noticed how unsettled they appeared.

"He's still alive right?" he asked in a tone that was barely above a whisper."

"Yea, he keeps nodding off tho," Tre answered.

"It doesn't look that bad," Rugged said while walking towards them.

"Tre and Butta, yall go home and stay there aight?"

"No getting on the phone and sayin shit! No going outside to the wall and saying shit. Yall get your stories straight if Popo comes around."

"Yea, we was all at Ro's watching videos," Butta, said.

"What about Lil Mickey? What we gonna say happened?" Ro asked Rugged.

"We'll figure that out on the way, let's go, he needs to go now."

Tre and Butta gave everyone a pound and a hug then headed home. Nature and Rugged each grabbed Lil Mickey by the arm and pulled him up. He let out a moan, opened his eyes and then closed them again. On the way to Montifiore emergency they all agreed on an alibi. If asked, Ro was to say that they were all at his house watching videos. Lil Mickey and Ro decided to walk to the store on Gun Hill Rd. since all of the stores in Foster were closed. On the way they were robbed at gunpoint, Lil Mickey didn't want to up any of his money so the robber shot him and ran. They have no idea what he looked like because he had his face covered.

CANCER

Cancer could barely see straight, he was so pissed off. Not only did he find out that Jada had lied to him about the whole birthday thing, he finds out that Calvin and his mother were killed and it's a good possibility that it was them bitch ass niggas from Foster who did it. Cancer knew Calvin was a hot head, that's why he liked him. He knew Calvin pushed that kid from Foster into on coming traffic a few nights ago, but so what thought Cancer. He was from Foster and deserved it strictly on that alone. He pulled on his cigarette then flicked it out the car window. "But to add insult to injury, I get home, take my shower, return some phone calls, handle some business then scan the news for any mention of Calvin and his mom's death and this bitch Keisha calls me."

Cancer stopped at the red light and looked to his right. He noticed that the driver in the car next to him was staring at him.

"What mutha fucka? You ain't neva talked to yourself before?" he barked.

The driver quickly turned away and as the light turned green, Cancer replayed the conversation he had with Keisha over in his head.

"First she nag me about not calling her back after having paged me at least five times earlier today. Then she gon tell me while sitting on her terrace she sees Terry's younger sister walk into A building. And how she had seen a little while earlier, Ro, Lil Mickey, Rugged and Nature leave."

"And knowing Romelo, he probably got that girl waiting for him on the roof. These little dumb bitches let them take they hot asses up to the roof and sex them, they nasty. At least let the nigga pay for a room, shit!"

"That's why I fuck with you Keisha," Cancer had said to her.

"Huh?" she asked sounding perplexed.

"Cause you have a big fucking mouth."

"Well you like when this big fucking mouth is sucking your big fucking dick don't you?" she asked and then broke out into a loud laugh. When Keisha noticed that he wasn't laughing she shut up.

"So you coming over Cancer?"

"Oh yea…I'm coming. I'm on my way," he said with a grin then hung up the phone.

ROMEL0

Nature pulled up to the Emergency room entrance. He glanced at Lil Mickey through the rear view and noticed his eyes were open. They had managed to keep him talking the entire ride. Rugged gave him and Romelo the scenario and made them repeat it over and over again.

"What happened to you Lil Mickey?" he asked him again.

"Me and Ro was going to the store...and we got robbed. Ro gave up his dough...but I didn't want to so I...got popped."

"Where was yall going Ro?"

"To the store at Gun Hill cause all the stores over here were closed. He approached us from behind and no we don't know what he look like cause his face was covered. Now can we get him inside?"

"Yea, I'm gon park here Rugged, leave the car and catch a cab. Yall admit him and then bounce," said Nature.

They got out the car and helped Lil Mickey to his feet. Lil Mickey put one arm around Ro's neck and the other around Rugged's. Nature watched them as they approached the automatic sliding doors that led to the emergency area. Once they were no longer in his eyesight he turned around to hail a cab.

"Nature?" Ro yelled as he was running up to him.

"What?"

"Don't forget. Go get her."

"Ok ok man, okay. Don't worry i'm going now, just hurry up."

Nature looked up and down the block but couldn't spot a cab anywhere in sight. He walked to the pay phone and called one instead. He then decided to call Nae Nae to hip her to what was happening and make sure everything was ok.

"Hello?" she answered sounding heated.

"What up Nae? Everything alright?"

"Naw Nature, the damn phone won't stop ringing."

"Who calling?"

"Everyone and they damn daddy. Girls calling saying they heard Ro was dead. Butta called twice wanting to speak to Ro, saying he seen the story on the news. And the police just left too."

"What? PoPo was there? Damn! What did they want?"

"They asked for Ro. First they asked for Trevor and I said there's no Trevor here. Then they asked for Romeo. I said I don't know a Romeo Jones. Then they spelled his name."

"Then what?"

"I said I didn't know where he was. What happened with Lil Mickey? He gonna be ok?"

"I'm on my way, I don't wanna talk no more on this phone, you neva know who else is listening nawmean?"

"Yea, that's true."

"Nae you think that girl is up there on the roof waiting for Ro?"

"I don't know Nature just come on and then go get her if she is."

"Aight, here go my cab now. Yo Nae, don't answer the door no more. Wait till I get there."

"Ok," Nae Nae replied.

Nature hung up the phone and thought about everything Nae Nae just told him.

"Shit!" he said aloud.

The cab driver honked his horn and startled Nature. He walked swiftly to the cab and got in.

"Where to?" the driver asked.

"Take me to 4200 Hutchinson, to Foster."

JADA

Monica's mother insisted on staying behind and helping Reggie and Mary clean up. Monica asked her mother for the keys, so she could throw the camcorder and some other stuff in the backseat. She told her after that she was going to walk Jada home.

"I will be right back mommy," she said while palming the car keys.

Monica looked for Jada; she found her standing with the DJ. And Shonda. They were talking about all the sirens they heard earlier. Monica made eye contact with her best friend and held up the car keys. Jada smiled and mouthed the words," I'm coming."

She walked over to her mother and gave her a huge hug.

"Thanks again Mommy. Thanks for everything," she said while smiling at her father.

"Your welcome baby. You sure you don't wanna hang around? We can all drive home together."

"Naw, me and Monie are going to hang out a lil while longer, show off these beautiful dresses. I'll be home soon though, I promise. Is daddy gonna be there when I get there?"

"Yea, he's gonna help me carry all those gifts home, and I know you want all these balloons too. Besides, he's not leaving for North Carolina until monday morning. So yes he will be there," Mary said sheepishly.

"Good. Cause when I get home we got some talking to do."

Jada went over to her father, who was helping himself to another serving of chicken, and kissed him on his cheek.

"See you later daddy."

"Ok baby gurl, I love you," he said between chews.

She met Monica at the door and tried to hide her excitement, but couldn't. "Let's go, let's go, lets go!"

"Told you I could get the keys."

She drove straight to Foster houses and teased Jada the whole way.

"Now yall don't be doing anything up on that roof that I wouldn't do."

"Were not...we just want to spend a little time together on my birthday. Talk about getting married, you know stuff like that."

"Now you know yall gonna do more then talk."

"No Monie were not," Jada said with a giggle.

"Ummm hmmmm."

"Ok, maybe kiss."

Both girls laughed hard.

"Now which way do I go?" Monica asked once they were out of Vector.

"Umm let me see...oh ok make a right here and then go straight."

"Are we in Foster now?" She asked after having driven a few blocks.

"Yea, this is Foster.'

"You know Jay, this is the first time I have ever actually been inside of Foster. It don't look no different then Vector. The buildings are bigger, taller and that's about it. I wonder who started all that crap about Foster and how they think they are better then us."

"I don't know Monie but its stupid and I wish it would end. People we know and love are losing they lives over what? A piece of ground that no one living here even owns?" Jada said angrily.

"Word. Is this it right here?" Monica asked while peering out the window.

"Yea. Ok how do I look?"

"You still look beautiful Jada. You sure you don't want me to walk you?"

"I'm okay, it's the big red building right there."

Jada got out the car and slammed the door. She leaned in the window and smiled at Monica.

"Thanks Monie. I'm a call you when I get home. I love you."

"Yea you make sure you call me and I love you too girl."

Monica watched Jada walk to the big red building she now knew to be A building. She watched her until she saw Jada go inside the front doors and head towards the elevators. Jada entertained the thought of going to Apt.5e first and surprising Ro but he had said to meet him on the roof, so that's where she headed. As she rode the elevator all the way up to the 26th floor She began to feel butterflies in her stomach. It was amazing to her, that just the thought of Romelo Jones could make her feel this way, all mushy inside.

"Chill girl," she said to herself.

Jada thought back on the day and how wonderful it has been. She figured she had to be the happiest person on the planet right about now.

"I got gifts, got to see my father and now Ro."

When Jada opened the door leading to the roof she peeked out, hoping to find Romelo waiting on her. She didn't, but what she did find was a blanket laid out, two unlit candles, a small radio, his poetry book, a single rose, a bottle of some unknown wine and two cups lying on top of the blanket. Jada smiled.

"He hasn't had a chance to finish setting up," she thought. She walked over to the blanket and picked up the rose, Jada bought it to her nose and inhaled. She then rubbed the soft petals on her cheek.

"He is so sweet," she said. She placed the rose back down. She bent down and pressed play on his radio, "Meeee anddd Missus Missus Jonessss," sang out. Jada pressed stop and laughed out loud. She picked up Romelo's book of poetry. She ran her fingers across his name, which was written in ink on the cover. Jada flipped through it, not wanting to invade what he may consider private, until she found a blank page with a pencil hiding between the sheets. She wrote,

Dear Romelo,
I have never experienced anything like this.
I know were both young but that saying is true.
Age ain't nuthin but a number. I love you with all my heart.
And I can't wait for the day when I become Mrs. Jada Jones.
Eventually we will say goodbye to Foster and Vector
But we will let them know, all the fighting, all the arguing,
All the killing, it couldn't keep true love apart.
I love you Ro- Jay.

She closed the book and laid it back down on the blanket. She then walked over to the small railing, leaned over and peered down on Foster.

"OH ROMEO ROMEO, WHEREFORE ART THOU ROMEO?" she yelled.

"LET ME BE YOUR JULIET." Jada giggled and walked back to the blanket. She sat down, pulled her knees up to her chin and waited on her Romeo.

CANCER

Cancer pulled up in front of building A in Foster. He looked up to the roof and frowned. He put the car in park and picked up the little velvet box that was lying on the seat beside him. He placed it in his jacket pocket and then picked up the gun that had been lying next to the box. He put that in his other pocket and went to A building. He hoped Keisha wasn't still minding everybody's business while sitting on her terrace. He didn't have time to deal with her right now. He knew she wasn't going to take the news that he didn't want to be with her anymore, to well. Cancer walked quickly to the front doors and pushed open the broken security door. Once inside the elevator, Cancer began to feel the disdain he had for Foster rise. He climbed the one flight of stairs leading to the roof quietly, the whole time his hand was jammed into his pocket, holding on to his gun. He pushed the roof door open and the first thing he spotted was Jada. He stood there for a few seconds and eyed her. Cancer's lips drew up into a scowl and he finally spoke, "Happy Birthday Jada."

Jada, startled and believing it to be Romelo, scrambled to her feet and spun around.

"Romelo!'

Once she realized who it was her smile faded.

"Cancer? What are you doing here?"

"I came to give you your gift Jay. Don't you want it?"

Cancer took a few steps closer to Jay and instincts told her to take a few steps back from him. Cancer looked at the ground; he saw the rose first and then the candles.

"Looks like i'm interrupting something Jay."

He looked her up and down, the sight of her standing there under the moonlight looking never more beautiful then she did at this very moment caused him to have mixed emotions. He hated her for being here and yet he loved her, always had.

"Damn you look good Jay."

"Thank you. Cancer?"

"How was the party?"

"Cancer look…" Jada tried.

"No Jay don't. Cause i'm not gonna understand. See I don't understand why you lied to me, why you played me and is continuing to play me right now," he said.

"Cancer cant we talk later, I'm…I'm waiting for someone."

"Who you waiting for Jay?" he asked, his voice raising.

Jay began to fear Cancer. She looked him in his eyes; he didn't seem to be the same person she thought she knew. Were all those nasty rumors she had heard about him true? She wondered.

"You waiting for that punk mutha fucka Romelo? I don't believe this shit!" Cancer walked over to the blanket and kicked the rose. Jada watched it skid across the ground and come to a halt near the wall.

"How you gonna be disloyal to Vector? How you gonna be disloyal to me Jay?"

179

"Cancer I don't owe you nuthin. Granted you have been here for me and my mother but..."

"Oh yea you do Jay," he said angrily.

He walked towards her with a look of disgust on his face.

"You owe me ma."

He stepped in front of her and just stared at her. Jada was truly frightened, but more for Romelo then herself. She silently prayed that he wouldn't come through that door.

"Cancer please...you're scaring me."

He reached into his pocket and pulled out the small box. Jay looked down at his hand and couldn't believe her eyes.

"I love you Jay and in time I want you to be my wife."

He reached out to touch her cheek and saw her pull away from his touch.

"What? What's that? You not gonna say yea Jay?" he yelled.

"No...no cancer, i'm not..."

"I know you love me, you call me, we chill wit each other."

"Cancer you're like a brother to me...ever since Terry died, that's how I see you. I thought..."

"Oh! He said while turning his back on her. "Oh! Oh!" he then began to laugh out loud.

"You thought I was doing all of that strictly out of the kindness of my fuckin heart?"

Cancer walked over to the roof railing and looked down. Jada stood there in shock, almost afraid to move. She watched him shake his head back and forth and then he turned to face her again.

"You fucked him?

She didn't answer.

"Yea you did…its ok I forgive you baby," he said, his smile growing larger.

Jada shook her head in disbelief.

"Cancer what I do or whom I'm with is my business."

"So whut you saying Jada? You not tryna be with me?"

"Cancer i'm not in love with you. I'm…" Jada took a deep breath and looked at Cancer with apprehension.

"I'm in love with Romelo. I mean I have love for you but I…"

"Shut up! Shut up! Shut da fuck up Jay! You ain't nothing but a hoe!"

Jada was startled by Cancer's outburst, she had never heard him yell or even curse before. He backed away from the railing and looked at the small box. Cancer then threw the tiny box as far as he could; he followed it with his eyes until he couldn't see the velvet box any longer.

"Fuck it!" He looked at her with a sorry expression on his face. "Fuck it Jay." He reached into his pocket and pulled out his gun.

"What is that for Cancer?" Jay asked in shock.

"I don't know Jay…I'm sayin, I feel like you being a bitch, standing here telling me all this bullshit. You actin like…like you crazy or something. Like you done lost your mind or some shit."

Cancer held the gun down near his thigh and began to walk towards Jada.

NATURE

Nature took his time climbing the steps. He really didn't expect to see Jada standing up there waiting on Romelo. He pushed the door open and walked out onto the rooftop. Nature did indeed see Jada, but he also saw Cancer standing in front of her with his back to the door. Jada's eyes opened even wider at the sight of Nature, this caused Cancer to spin around. When he did Nature caught a full glimpse of the gun he held in his hand.

"What da fuck is this?" He asked in disbelief, eyes darting from Jay to Cancer.

"You was tryna ambush my brotha? I tried to tell him not to trust any bitch from Vector."

"Nature wait, it's not like that, I was supposed to meet Ro here, we planned this. It's my birthday," Jada explained.

"Then what da fuck you doing here?" he asked Cancer.

"I'm waiting for Romelo also, but you know what? I'm glad you're here cause now I can kill two birds with one mutha fuckin stone.

ROMELO

Rugged walked from the payphone back to the emergency waiting room where he had left Ro. He saw him talking to a cop so he bent down untied both his sneakers then retied them, read something on the bulletin board about teen age pregnancy, went to the vending machine, got a soda then headed back to Ro, who was now sitting alone.

"What did he want?"

"Questioning me about the robbery," Ro answered.

"Again?"

"Word."

"I don't like this...don't feel right. Nae said 5oh been to the crib asking for you and Tre. We need to bounce man. How's Lil Mickey?"

"Doctor said it was a bullet that went straight through him. Didn't hit any major arteries so looks like he gon be alright."

"Kool, lets go," Rugged said while rising up out of his seat.

"Did Nature get Jay yet?"

"Nae said she spoke to him on the phone earlier and he said he was gonna go get her so..."

Romelo stood up and looked at the dry bloodstains on his hoodie.

"Man, I just wanna go home, take this off so bad, hop in the shower, change and see Jay."

They walked towards the emergency exit.

"Gammy is ok right?"

"Yea Nae said she don't know nuthin."

"Good, she doesn't need to know. Don't want her getting upset."

Rugged unlocked the car door and let Ro in. Once inside, Ro looked at Rugged with wide eyes.

"Rugged, what you thinks gonna happen?" he asked him.

"I don't know man. I mean I ain't gonna sugarcoat it. You may have to leave New York for a minute. You alright wit dat?"

"I guess i'm gonna hafta be right?"

"Right."

Rugged put the car in drive and they headed back to Foster.

NATURE

"What dat supposed to mean, killing two birds?" Nature asked Cancer.

"What chu think it means? Nigga I want you dead, I want your brother dead, I want all you pussy mutha fucka's in Foster dead. Not because of what yall did today, but just for g.p."

Cancer raised his gun and pointed it at Nature.

"Cancer stop!" Jay yelled.

"Baby gurl, either go down stairs to my car or turn your back, you don't wanna see this."

"If you gon do it, then just do it nigga! What's all the talking for? Pop me, but you ain't poppin Ro." Nature said with both his arms stretched out.

Cancer laughed out loud.

"Dat nigga killed Calvin and his family today, and you telling me i'm not gonna blow his fuckin head off?"

"What?" Jay asked.

"You not, Ro is already dead," Nature said flatly.

"What?" Jay asked again.

"That's what I came up here to tell you. One your your boys from Vector shot him. That's why he ain't here now Jay. His last words to me was,' go to the roof, get Jay and tell her that I'm sorry.'

"No...no, you are lying. I don't believe you," Jay said.

"Well that's on you, I'm just doing what my brother asked me to do."

"Well your family betta purchase two caskets cause they gonna be mourning both of yall," Cancer said while pointing the gun at Nature.

Jada couldn't believe what she was hearing. She suddenly felt nothing but hate and disgust for both Nature and Cancer. At this very moment she didn't care if either one of their worlds ended because her's just did. It just stopped revolving. She looked at Cancer again and decided that she couldn't stand here and let him murder Ro's brother, so Jay threw herself at him with all her strength; she tried to knock the gun out of his hand. Both of her hands hit his arm, causing her and the gun to hit the ground. Before Cancer could figure out what had happened, Nature rushed him, growling the whole time. He pushed Cancer back to the railing and landed on top of him. Nature bought his fist all the way from South Carolina and made contact with Cancer's nose. Blood squirted out his nose like water from out of a water gun. Nature raised his fist to do it again but Cancer quickly jerked his head to the side, causing Nature fist this time to make contact with concrete. Nature yelled out in pain. Cancer wrestled his way out from under Nature and quickly stood and kicked him in the back. Nature fell face down on the pavement. Cancer raised his foot and kicked Nature in the back of his head. Nature grabbed Cancer's pants leg with his left hand and pulled hard. Cancer lost his footing and fell to the pavement next to him. Nature grabbed Cancer, Cancer grabbed at him. They rolled and grunted and tried to kill each other with their bare hands until they heard someone yelling.

"Stop! Stop! Stop!"

They both stopped and turned their heads in the direction of the yelling. Jada stood above them with the gun pointed at the both of them. She had tears streaming down her face and her hands were shaking terribly.

"Just stop it!" she whimpered.

Nature got to his feet, so did Cancer and they stood side by side, both staring at Jay."

"Jay, give me the gun," Nature insisted.

"No!" she said while taking a few steps back from them.

"Don't you understand what you just did to me?" she asked.

"You gonna tell me that Romelo's dead? My world…my life? The only person that brings me happiness is gone?" Jay wiped the tears that had gathered at the tip of her chin off. She felt as if she was going to faint.

"Why Cancer?" she asked while looking at him.

He responded only with a blank stare.

"Why Nature?" she asked while staring him down.

"Jay. Just gimmie the gun. After that we can go and talk," Nature tried.

"Why God?" she yelled out loud. "I know I'm not supposed to question you but why?" she let out a moan that was heart wrenching. She felt nauseous and was about to drop down to her knees; she lowered her head and the gun. Cancer took one step towards her and she quickly raised both again.

"Get away from me!" she yelled.

"You're the reason why he's dead! Both of yall! Vector, Foster I'm tired of this shit! I have been hearing this, going through this my whole life! Foster!

Vector! Foster! Vector! Foster! Vector! Yall the reason why Terry's not here now. Why my dad jumps every time he hears an ambulance siren. Why my mother gets petrified if i'm out when the sun goes down."

"You can't put that on us," Cancer said.

"We didn't make the streets, the streets made us."

Jada gave Cancer an empty stare.

"This is how it's always been and how its gonna always be, "Nature said.

Jada shook her head, "Yall wrong, me and Ro knew just how wrong yall are. What am I supposed to do now? We were gonna get married..." Jada trailed off.

Cancer made a noise that sounded like a laugh.

"How many bullets in here Cancer? Huh? Enough for all three of us?"

"Ok, you buggin now," he said with a sly smile.

"Go," she said as she walked around them.

"Huh?" Nature asked.

"GO! Get the fuck out! This is our place and I don't want yall here!"

Jada now stood behind them.

"Jay please...just come with me," Nature said, his back to her.

"Go!" she yelled again.

And with that both Nature and Cancer began to walk towards the exit door. They both suddenly stopped dead in their tracks when they heard the sound of a gun go off. Nature spun around and watched Jada fall to the rooftop ground.

"Oh No!" he yelled.

Cancer turned around slowly; he took one look at Jada and then dropped his head.

Romelo was feeling a little bit better; he had taken off his blood soaked clothes and quickly showered and changed. He couldn't understand what was taking Nature and Jay so long, so he decided to head up to the roof to see. He sprinted up the steps and heard the unmistakable sound of a single gunshot. His heart began to beat a mile a minute as he took on the last few remaining steps. When Ro pushed open the door that led to the roof, he was greeted by the sight of Nature and Cancer, who both had their backs to him. They stood there looking down at something; Ro wondered what it could be.

"What happened?" he asked.

He had meant for it to come out loud enough for either one of them to hear and respond but it didn't, it was just a faint whisper. Still standing in the doorway, Ro stretched his neck and tried to look around Nature, He caught a glimpse of someone's feet.

"What happened?" he asked again. This time managing to have the words come out louder then a whisper. He parted Nature and Cancer by stepping in between both of them.

"Wait Ro!" Nature said. He grabbed him by the shoulder and tried to prevent him from getting any closer. Ro slowly turned his head and looked his brother in the eyes. Nature met his eyes with a look of grief on his face. He then turned to look at the ground and he saw her. Jada was lying there on her back, eyes close. He could see a large burgundy spot on her dress but he couldn't tell from where it came.

"Nature? What happened?" He asked, still looking down at her.

"She shot herself Ro."

189

"No she didn't! Why? Why would she do that?" Ro asked.

No one answered him.

Ro fell to his knees beside her as the tears filled his eyes.

"Jay?"

He put his hand on her forehead and moved away a few strands of hair that lay there.

"Oh my god...you look so beautiful. Jay? Wake up ok? I got something to tell you..."

Her eyes fluttered and then Jada opened her eyes. She looked up at Ro and smiled.

"Hey Romelo Jones," she whispered.

"Hey Jada Jones, happy birthday boo," he said with a faint smile.

"We made it huh?" she asked.

Romelo bent down and kissed her on her lips.

She smiled again and closed her eyes.

He reached for her hand and noticed she still had the gun in it. He pried it from her fingers and looked at it. He then looked up at Nature and Cancer and the tears fell down his cheeks. Jada started breathing harder, her chest lifted up and went down at a faster pace now. She opened her eyes again and asked for Ro.

"I'm right here Jay," he whispered in her ear.

"Read me one of your poems please?" She asked, her chest still rising and coming down at a faster pace. He lifted her head up and placed it on his lap.

"There's a rose growing in the Bronx," he began.

It was clear that Jay was having a hard time breathing. Her breath intakes were quick and short. A tear fell from Ro's face and landed on her forehead.

"That's something that's rarely seen..." he continued.

She looked up at Ro and took her last breath. When Ro noticed that he didn't feel her breathing any longer he took his hand and placed it over her eyes, he gently closed them. He then raised the hoodie he was wearing up over his head and the gun fell out, landing next to him. Ro slowly and carefully folded his hoodie and placed it on the pavement. He lifted Jay's head from off his legs and placed it on his sweat hood.

"I love you," he said.

Nature walked over to him and helped him up.

"I'm sorry Ro," he said. He then grabbed Romelo and hugged him. Ro's arms just hung freely to his side, he didn't return the embrace.

"Where Cancer go?"

"That son of a bitch ran out a few minutes ago," Nature said while looking at the open exit door.

"You aight?" He asked Ro after letting him go.

"No...I loved her Nature." He turned around and looked at her again.

"C'mon Ro, lets go man."

"Go where?" Ro asked his brother.

"Home," he said while trying to get his brother to exit the roof.

"Home?...ok just give me a minute."

"OK, i'm a be at the elevator."

Nature stood for a few seconds and looked at Ro. He didn't like what he saw. Ro just had a blank look on his face, no emotion. He turned and started for the exit.

Romelo bent down and picked up the gun that had fell out of his hoodie, the one Jay used just minutes ago. He sat down next to her, took her hand, placed the gun in his mouth and pulled the trigger. Nature stopped right in front of the door when he heard the shot. He didn't even bother to turn around, he fell to his knees and beat his fist on his head.

"OH NO...NO...GOD NOOOO!!" he repeated over and over again.

EPILOUGE

Jada Romain was pronounced dead on her 16th birthday. Romelo Jones was also listed as a DOA, eight years after having first crossed paths with the love of his life. The deaths were determined to be a double suicide. Police confiscated the handgun that was used in the suicides and found it had been used in two previous murders. One in Brooklyn the other in East Orange New Jersey. Wendell "Cancer" Felter was arrested in connection with the East Orange murder and is currently calling Rikers Island his home, while awaiting trail.

Tanaesha became so distraught after hearing the news of her baby brothers death that she want into premature labor. She gave birth to a four-pound 6oz. baby boy. She named him Romelo. After graduation she and Rahiem "Rugged" Campbell left Foster houses. They moved to a neighborhood in California that appeared to be war free. It took Nae Nae and Rugged just two short weeks to find out that they now reside in the middle of another war. Only difference is this one is not about where you live but what colors you rep.

Nathaniel "Nature" Jones still lives in Apt 5e in Foster houses with his grandmother. Two days after Romelo's funeral, a mural appeared behind A building.

It reads," R.I.P. RO AND JAY. YALL MADE IT OUT."

No one knows who painted it but Nature can be found sitting by it on many a night. Sometimes drinking, sometimes talking to himself or writing poetry.

Randie "Butta" Gardner, Trevor "Tre" Smith, and "Lil" Mickey Robson were all arrested for the murders of Calvin and Carol Smith. Lil Mickey copped a plea bargain with the State of New York and testified against Butta and Tre. Lil Mickey was given a 6-month suspended sentence, while Butta and Tre each were hit with a 7-14 bid. Lil Mickey's mother, out of fear for her son's life moved him and the rest of her family out of Foster.

The following year, Monica Ramsey graduated from high school. She managed to get the entire senior class to wear pink ribbons on their gowns, in memory of her best friend Jada. After graduation, Monica got a tattoo on her upper arm that reads, 'Jada my best friend forever.' She is currently studying communications at Howard University.

Mary Romain didn't attend her daughter's funeral. She remained at home, under heavy sedation and watched closely by family and friends. She eventually packed up Jada's things and gave them to charity. She foreclosed the house at 1680 Thornwood Drive and moved to Charlotte, North Carolina. Her and Reggie remarried and are living a quiet existence.

The Foster/Vector war continues to this day.

ABOUT THE AUTHOR

First time author, Tasha Campbell grew up in the Bronx, New York. After graduating from Truman High School, she went on to attend and graduate from the City College of New York, with a major in communications. Tasha Campbell has had poetry and magazine article's published but this is her first novel. She is currently working on a second one. Tasha Campbell currently resides in Charlotte, North Carolina.